'When I first met Dare she was a very conf
point when she would have nipped out of
who was fully on her side. I have watched Dare ~~~~
Heather's sympathetic hands, never pushing her beyond her limitations and
always encouraging her every step of the way. She's now a happy, confident
little dog because Heather had it in her to give her the chance she so needed. I
applaud Heather for giving her the chance she so longed for and never judging
her while helping her every step of the way. If everyone had it in them to
rescue a scared, confused little dog the world would be a brighter place'

Linda Rutherford, three times Crufts Obedience winner

'Three years ago, on a dark and cold March evening I was introduced to Dare.
Heather opened the van doors and I saw huddled at the back of the cage a very
frightened and confused looking little hairy dog. Heather had explained that
she had picked her up and was taking her to her new home in Scotland. Don't
ask me why for I do not know, but I knew then that this little girl was staying
with Heather. Heather eventually coaxed this bundle of fear out of the van.
Dare's eyes were dull and untrusting, her coat dry and sparse, her tail was
tucked so tight under her body she looked like she had been docked. She could
not have slinked closer to the ground if she had tried. I could not look at her
without feeling sad. She was so worried and had no idea about what was
happening to her. Heather in my eyes was already smitten. What was to
happen to this little dog who only wanted to be loved and understood. When I
got the news that the home she was supposed to go to did not work out and
that Heather had decided to keep her I was so pleased. I still remember that
night, but now when I look into Dare's eyes I see contentment and trust. She is
loved and cared for in a way that she deserves and who better to give her a
forever home than Heather Smith. Bless you Dare, you are the hope that all
dogs can be given a chance to show what they can become with kindness, love
and patient handling. From wags to riches I would say'   Gill Crawford, K9
Pursuits

DARE'S DIARY

From Rescue Dog to Crufts and Beyond

Heather Smith

Dare's Diary by Heather Smith

ISBN: ISBN-13: 978-1977535450 (CreateSpace-Assigned)
ISBN-10: 1977535453

DEDICATION

For Dare who fills my life with such joy and happiness and without whom there would be no Diary

Dare's Diary by Heather Smith

Dare's Diary by Heather Smith

ACKNOWLEDGMENTS

My thanks to my family and friends who have encouraged and supported me in writing this book.

I am eternally thankful to Ellen Bothwick for taking me through the publishing process and to Penny Mansfield and Anne Stewart who have read my drafts and offered feedback.

I'd also like to thank Michelle Porter for her continued support and training with Dare.

Finally, my thanks to the many others who have contributed with information about Dare and her background including Rachel Walker's family. My thoughts are frequently on Rachel who I didn't know but who was Dare's first companion and who took Dare on her first step of her journey. I hope you can see Dare from Heaven, Rachel.

Dare's Diary by Heather Smith

1 IN THE BEGINNING

This book is inspired by Dare's Diary, a little coffee stained notebook of thoughts and plans I kept in the first years of living with Dare. I never intended it to be anything other than a prompt to my memory and it quickly filled up with a 'To do' list as well as with my worries and concerns about Dare and her behaviour. Over time I started to write about the positives in our days, always trying to find two or three of these each day and with Dare they started to become easier and easier to find so often starting with the many aspects of her loving nature and progressing to her achievements in overcoming her fears and worries.

I can't put into words what it was in Dare that drew me to her and if I am completely honest her looks must have played a part. She was advertised on Facebook as needing a home and unusually I commented on the picture as she reminded me of my first rescue working bearded collie, Skye. And when I met her, in the process of helping in her rehoming to Scotland, I most certainly could feel something in her which drew me to her. I am certain that this wasn't pity for the situation she found herself in, nor was it that I felt she could become a top competition dog. As corny and unscientific (as someone speaking with such a background) as this sounds I believe it was love at first sight and for the first weeks I told myself ……. 'She isn't yours', 'Do not get attached', 'You have five dogs already and that's enough for anyone to care for and spend time with'.

I'd like to say from the very onset that this is in no way a training manual, and despite being a dog trainer I have never been tempted to write such a book. Each dog is so much an individual and Dare is no exception to this. As such every action I have taken with her has been with Dare and her unique personality and needs in mind. Of course, there are universals in dog training but on the whole and with all my dogs, I have spent time observing them and attempted to assess and see their personalities and treat them as the distinct individuals that they are – in getting to know your dog and gauging your dog's normal baseline behaviour you will have a fabulous starting point from which to train any dog. I hold a strong belief that each dog should be viewed and trained with a holistic approach, thus not dealing with any issue or training exercise as isolated from the dog's complete being. I hope this will be evident as Dare's story with me unfolds and the various threads in Dare's life that we worked on together merge into a happier dog.

Every dog I have lived with has taught me something but there is no dog that I have learnt so much from as Dare. This is the gift that dogs with challenges bring to you.

I am lucky to have Dare in my life, but this came at the cost of her previous owner Rachel Walker's death in January 2014. I never met Rachel but have been fortunate enough to meet both her Dad and her sister and speak to people who knew her. Rachel took on Dare from Wiccaweys Rescue Centre and knew that Dare had been brought their from Ireland.

Rachel's dad, Tony May spoke to me about Rachel and her dogs,

'Rachel obtained Dare to be a companion for Chaos, her Belgian Shepherd. Rachel's passion   was obedience training and competitions and Rachel and Chaos were getting quite successful and winning rosettes. Dare was the most loving dog, although scared silly of most noises. With Rachel receiving treatments for cancer poor Dare did not receive all the help she needed getting over her fears. Dare was also very wary of men, although great with me. Rachel's, first and our family dog, Bramble came from a RSPCA centre when Rachel was about ten years old and a lot of our Sundays were spent going to charity dog shows and entering junior handler classes with Bramble. Dogs were Rachel's passion; her dream was to have a dog training business one day. I promised I would find homes for Chaos and Dare when she passed away. Rachel was diagnosed with breast cancer just a couple of years after her mum died and passed away only eleven years later.'   Tony May

One thing that stays firmly in my mind is Rachel's commitment to difficult dogs as Dare wasn't her first 'problem child', she named her fearful girl Dare in the hope that she lived up to her name and I was touched by her words on her blog speaking as her beloved DareDog:

'one day I might win Crufts or something'

I am honoured to have fulfilled her ambition for Dare in getting her to Crufts and beyond, and who knows what the future may bring as Dare's story hasn't reached an ending yet. I consider Dare as Rachel's gift to me, and I am sure she is a part of who Dare is.

2 AND SO THE JOURNEY BEGINS

Adverts for dogs needing homes on social media do concern me. Whilst I appreciate the wide reach that such adverts have in helping find homes for dogs such as Dare, they are not without pitfalls. The adverts are not always accurate in their descriptions of the dogs and tend to avoid the difficulties that the dog may bring with him or her. This can result in people taking on dogs which are unsuitable for their lifestyle or which may be behaviourally challenging as they have picked the dog for his/her looks. In Dare's case she was the cute hairy dog!

Dare's advert appeared on Facebook with a picture of a dog that reminded me of Skye, my first rescue Bearded Collie. Unusually I did comment on the post, but I was not looking to expand my canine family. As with all such adverts I really hoped that this lovely dog could be found a home.

Following Rachel's death Dare found herself in the care of Nicky Mackie. Nicky had visited Rachel's parents to pick up her other dog, a Belgian Shepherd Dog, Chaos on behalf of his breeder. Nicky described arriving and not knowing about Dare who was in a kitchen until she started creating havoc and barking. As Nicky approached her, Dare flew at her from behind her gate but stopped when Nicky turned side on to her thereby appearing less threatening. Nicky offered to take Dare to rehome too as she felt she wouldn't cope in kennels. I think this is very likely to have been the case as Dare was rescued from Wiccaweys Border Collie Rescue Kennels by Rachel and at the time just prior to their investigation by the RSPCA for keeping dogs in unacceptable conditions. Dare was to be lucky in life yet again to have fallen into understanding and caring hands in the form of Nicky.

Nicky describes Dare as being more settled in her house and with her dogs where she enjoyed running with her eight Belgian Shepherds and rounding them up. Fortunately, Nicky's dogs are well behaved so ignored Dare's herding behaviour, but it was behaviour I was to recognise well when she came to live with me, and of course not all dogs will tolerate this behaviour, nor is it fair to expect them to.

Dare got along well with Rachel's dad and step mum but apparently was not good with their grandchildren hence she was in the kitchen behind a gate. The description of Dare 'nappy nipping' conjured up images that were far from positive in my mind. With Nicky's extensive understanding of dogs, she also talked about the effect of grief on a dog and said that with both Dare and Chaos she could see the dogs 'visibly change in front of your eyes when she took them home with 'No grief [to deal with] in my house'. The tragic death of Rachel clearly and understandably caused both dogs to grieve and feel her loss too.

It was a lady who had previously attended some of my classes that decided to give Dare a home alongside her other dogs. She had had worked with a Bearded Collie before and Dare clearly held appeal for her with her scruffy hairy looks. Of course, Dare at this point was living in Cornwall with Nicky and the new owner was hundreds of miles away in Scotland. She asked if I would get involved and pick up Dare from Crufts to save a long journey. I had never been involved in transporting a rescue dog before, but I agreed.

The arrangements seemed very straightforward. I was to pick Dare up from Nicky after my final day at Crufts and deliver her to her new home in Scotland.

3 CRUFTS 2014

It had been another exciting Crufts for me with my third win with Maddie in the Heelwork to Music final and our places in both the Freestyle Final and in the International Freestyle, where we represented Scotland. Following all this excitement I contacted Nicky to arrange the next stage of Dare's journey across Britain, from Cornwall to Scotland.

Nicky arrived with Dare at one of the exits outside of Crufts for me to collect. Dare was very edgy and energetic and clearly not settled, in short there was nervousness about her from which fear emanated. As I took her and started walking towards my van my first impressions were of her scooting about on the end of her lead jumping from my left to my right side and pulling here and there. She was clearly fearful of the traffic on the quiet road behind the Exhibition Centre in Birmingham and her radar like ears were moving up and down, back and forwards at all the sounds.

Then like a bolt from the blue, she almost pulled me over. We were also close to the airport and an airplane had went over our heads and in her fearful state she tried to slip her collar and lead and to escape, she followed this up very shortly afterwards by a similar reaction to a train. I could see why she was on a very tight collar – poor Dare was desperate to take flight from these sounds and she was trying to get her head out of her collar. It became increasingly clear over her first weeks with me that this was a trick she'd perfected!

These fear reactions were too strong for her to hear me or listen to me. To attempt to get her to chill a little would have been in vain so we rapidly kept on walking towards my van with anyone watching likely forming the impression that Dare knew where she was going as she dragged me along. She must have looked like the naughtiest dog in attendance at Crufts. We got back to my van after a twenty minute or so walk and Dare hadn't toileted, sniffed or did anything a normal dog would have done presented with a walk which included grass and plenty to sniff. She just couldn't wait to get into the cage in my van when the doors were opened, and she desperately needed to settle and calm down. She looked exhausted and she was yawning with stress as she lay at the very back of the cage, making herself look as small as possible. I spoke to her to try to reassure her, but she offered no acknowledgement and her eyes looked so very sad. Some images just stay in your head and this is one of them that I can see so clearly as I write this years later.

I wasn't travelling home till the following day, so I had to decide as to whether to try to get Dare into the Travelodge we were staying at. It wasn't a difficult decision to make in leaving her in the cage in my van rather than have her join us, as I felt another environment to contend with might be a step too far. The Travelodge would be busy, and she would have to cope with so much from the lift, the noises from the corridor and so on. She was still struggling to cope with the fear of planes which were flying low over the Travelodge car park and she was also showing fear of my dogs with her reaction such that she displayed strong avoidance, looking away in an exaggerated manner. Sadly, she found nothing supportive in the presence of other dogs.

So, getting Dare into the cage was all too easy, every time she felt fearful she took flight to the van and the cage with me trailing behind. Feeling safe in her cage was certainly a problem when she didn't want to come out and even this early on the need to toilet seemed very low on Dare's agenda and this caused me so much concern, as she was clean in her cage…… did she never need to pee! She had decided the carpark was a place she didn't like at all and I was reluctant to force her and had no intention of dragging this scared dog on the end of a lead, so patience was the name of the game – sitting with my back to the cage with the door open waiting for her to come forward for a tasty titbit or because she herself wanted out. Mainly though she would come forward grab the titbit and rush to the back of the cage again, but I knew patience always bears rewards. Bites are common in fearful (and cornered) dogs and there were many occasions where it was clear that if forced Dare would most certainly have bitten. I had no intention of giving this fearful dog a bad name by forcing her into a situation where I was the cause of her biting.

There were many clues to Dare's issues that were glaringly obvious this early on. Her reaction on meeting my dogs as well as my travel companion, Michelle's dogs was that of fear. She offered exaggerated avoidance behaviours such as looking and moving away, and if too close she would freeze, and her body would tense. The freezing was a more worrying reaction than the flight behaviour offered in response to noise (as of course she was always on lead). I was concerned that this may escalate to a fight situation and of course she was going to live with dogs in her new home. The fight, flight, fear response Dare clearly experienced was such that she was obviously overwhelmed by the situation she found herself in, she was literally paralyzed with fear.

Our journey home involved a beach stop off at Lytham St Anne's with both Michelle's dogs and mine. It's always nice to walk somewhere other than motorway service stations when travelling even if it takes you somewhat off the direct route home. Dare was initially on a long line and it was clear that in certain contexts she would recall. There was certainly some herding type behaviour that was unacceptable and during which she was unable to listen. Then again, this was early days and why would this little girl, Dare listen to me, after all we had no history, no relationship, and of course I wasn't looking to build a relationship.... She wasn't to be mine!

Dare was certainly a good traveller which was as well on our long journey to Scotland. Aren't their always wonderful positives to be found in any situation!

Gill Crawford of K9 Pursuits Ltd met Dare in that Car park:

'Three years ago, on a dark and cold March evening I was introduced to Dare. Heather opened the van doors and I saw huddled at the back of the cage a very frightened and confused looking little hairy dog. Heather had explained that she had picked her up and was taking her to her new home in Scotland. Don't ask me why for I do not know, but I knew then that this little girl was staying with Heather. Heather eventually coaxed this bundle of fear out of the van. Dare's eyes were dull and untrusting, her coat dry and sparse, her tail was tucked so tight under her body she looked like she had been docked. She could not have slinked closer to the ground if she had tried. I could not look at her without feeling sad. She was so worried and had no idea about what was happening to her. Heather in my eyes was already smitten. What was to happen to this little dog who only wanted to be loved and understood. When I got the news that the home she was supposed to go to did not work out and that Heather had decided to keep her I was so pleased. I still remember that night, but now when I look into Dare's eyes I see contentment and trust. She is loved and cared for in a way that she deserves and who better to give her a forever home than Heather Smith. Bless you Dare, you are the hope that all dogs can be given a chance to show what they can become with kindness, love and patient handling. From wags to riches I would say'   Gill Crawford

4 NEW HOME

My hat goes off to anyone involved in rescuing and rehoming dogs, it's not easy and things often don't work out for a variety of reasons. It's a job I know I would be ill equipped for as I would find it impossible not to become attached and I would want to keep them all!

We arrived home from Crufts late on Sunday evening and the handover of Dare was to be put off until the Tuesday so she was to stay with me.

I set her up a cage in the kitchen where she'd be part of everything going on and covered the sides leaving only a view from the front – it was to be her safe cave. All my dogs are used to being in a cage as pups, it's necessary for shows and for travelling that they get used to a cage and it's useful if they ever have to stay with the vet. They find cages rather exciting and when one is assembled they all try to get in. This could have potentially been a disaster given Dare's freezing if confronted or hemmed in by another dog, but I could also see she was likely to guard the cage especially where food was concerned. So, a closed-door policy was order of the day if Dare was in her cage.

I can still see Dare's face on the Monday morning with her eyes filled with apprehension, not wanting to come out of her cage. No doubt she was trying to make sense of her new environment filled with the barking Bearded Collies, Bonnie and Gertie and their over excitement in the mornings as well as the quieter four-legged family members! I took the others out a walk and had to leave her –the cage door opens of course and in the company of another new stranger, my partner, Bob. Of course, she eventually came out when ignored, scooted outside to pee and dashed straight back in again!

Another concern was that she wasn't eating properly, and she was very thin. But of course, this wasn't meant to be my problem and I was hopeful that when she settled in her new home she'd eat better and gain a little weight.

It was a Tuesday afternoon when I set off to take Dare to her new home. I'd been sent a postcode and was surprised to find myself on an industrial estate. My first thoughts were that I had the wrong postcode but her new owner turned up on foot before I had the chance to phone her. Surprisingly Dare got out of her cage straight away but quickly became fearful of the train track about 300 yards away and was frantically attempting to get her head out of the collar. Without handling Dare and despite having two other rescues Dare was rejected as unsuitable. To say I felt stunned disbelief that this person had brought Dare hundreds of miles across the country only to reject her was an understatement.

That night Dare travelled to my Dog Dance class in East Kilbride and Michelle brought her into the class, albeit briefly... I doubt that her whole visit was more than ten minutes. She was rather afraid of the noises that this building makes (it has a creaky floor and ceiling for want of a better description) and was unsettled, avoiding dogs, trying to get behind chairs and clearly wanting out of the door. This was combined with her over friendly behaviour towards some of the people at the class. However, Dare has certainly the ability to capture hearts and one lady was particularly impressed by her and she posted on Facebook that night with her concerns as to what was going to happen to Dare.

Shortly after this post I was contacted by the new 'owner' saying she would give Dare a chance after all. So, it was arranged that Dare should be handed over on Thursday morning in a car park next to the beach in the local town of Irvine. Perhaps not such a bad idea to get the dogs in Dare's new home to meet her on neutral territory.

Dare came out of the van but wasn't keen to go to her new home. I was very saddened when I got back into my van to see in my rear wing mirror Dare being dragged across the car park looking so cowed and unhappy. I would never drag any dog anywhere and it is not conducive to building a relationship of trust.

It was back to Facebook that night after I received a message from a friend to tell me there was a post saying Dare had bitten one of the other dogs in her new home and had been bitten herself.

I don't often phone anyone after 9pm but it was around 10pm when I phoned to enquire about Dare. Dare's behaviour on a walk was reported as difficult and she was apparently unable to be with the other dogs in the house either on a walk or at home. In short after less than 12 hours in her new home she was being rejected – hardly time for her to settle after the upset and changes she'd been through in her life.

I felt in some way responsible for this dog, after all I'd got involved in rehoming her. She clearly couldn't stay in this home, as in my opinion the home was unsuitable. I offered to pick Dare up and look after her till a new home or trip back to Cornwall could be arranged but my offer was refused.

Needless to say, I had a sleepless night thinking about Dare, so the next morning I contacted Nicky. I was travelling on the Friday to the Highlands to deliver a Clicker Training Weekend, but it was arranged via the wonderful and patient Nicky Mackie that I should have Dare collected and, in my absence, that job fell to the equally wonderful Michelle Porter. Michelle was to have Dare until I returned after the weekend.

Dare spent a weekend in another new home with Michelle and her husband Timmy and their two dogs, Dexter, a Bullmastiff crossbreed and Jaxon, a Bichon Frise. Needless to say, she was still difficult to walk with all her pulling and jumping about when something scared her, but she settled for the main part in the house. Dare showed signs of getting along well with the very confident and completely unflappable Jaxon and a close relationship has blossomed between these two over the years.

5 SHE'S STAYING IN THIS NEW HOME

Obviously though my heart went out to Dare, I had spent time telling myself not to get attached and involved. Dare is the kind of dog that gives so much, she is both loving and needy but I did not need a sixth addition to my family of dogs. I like to ensure my dogs have two or three good walks a day, that I spend individual time with each one and I had two older dogs which take as much if not more time than the youngsters ….. Oh, and did I mention I had a youngster too! I wanted to give Dare a home and could see that the last thing this girl needed was another long journey back to Cornwall! In all honesty this dog tugged at my heartstrings and truth be told was already under my skin and making her way into my heart. I wish I could quantify and put into words exactly how I felt about Dare, but let's just say I went with my gut feeling that all would be well.

But of course, I had my long-suffering partner Bob to consider though fortunately he came around quickly. I think he was highly influenced by Dare's footballing skills. He would play with her when he came home from work and I am sure her needy nature made him feel very wanted! He just announced one day – 'Dare isn't going anywhere now is she?' She's clearly his kind of girl too!

So, Dare became family and joined my golden oldies, rescue Skye (age 16) and Bonnie (age 14), the dogs I was competing with Maddie (age 8), Gertie (age 4) and little Bichon Frise baby, DinkyDiva who was a year old.

My aim for Dare was to happily live with all my other dogs in my home as part of our family. The vast majority of her life would be spent in my home and she had to feel settled, comfortable and happy here. I described Dare to my friends at the time as my behavioural work in progress and my stated aims were to have a happy companion who would keep us company on walks, join in our games and generally enjoy life. Competition was not on my horizon!

I made a list of the issues we needed to address in Dare's Scruffy Diary, that coffee stained notebook. Most of these issued centred around home life as there wasn't much hope of her coping with any of the other issues that were arising when I took her walks if she was unable to cope at home.

The most pressing problem was her desire to live in her cage and given reports of her life prior to being rescued by Rachel it's likely she spent most of her days in a cage. She could not easily be cajoled out and it was evident to me that if forced or confronted she was scared enough that she would bite. It would be counter-productive to try to build trust whilst at the same time using force with Dare, so I was patient. I spent time encouraging her to come and eat titbits, mostly she would come forward grab the food and take it to the back of the cage. As she grew more confident she would come out to play with me or to cuddle up close but of course it didn't take much for her to flee back into the cage. There were so many triggers to this but primarily they involved sound sensitivities and I will deal with this in greater length in a chapter of its own but the list of sounds she feared was not only lengthy but seemed to include noises I couldn't pinpoint but you could see the fear in her radar like ears and of course in her expression and eyes.

I had another concern with her flight to the cage and it involved the other dogs. She already avoided looking at the other dogs and would look away in an exaggerated fashion. The picture of her with Michelle's Bearded Collie, Luna as a pup says it all as she was initially terrified of little Luna, though this was to be turned around as you can also see in the second picture. And of course, this picture was taken many months later when things had improved.

I was concerned that an incident would take place with one of the other dogs, probably Bonnie and/or Maddie who represented the old and the weak respectively when Dare was in one of her over aroused and fearful states and on the run to the cage. Of course, there was also the worry that one of the other dogs tried to get in the cage with her which necessitated the cage door being closed at times and a baby gate being installed in the kitchen. Safety of all the dogs had to be paramount.

Of course, there were positives and when Dare did come out of the cage she was very playful and that was a huge plus, as I knew I would be able to build a relationship using this which would be more powerful than simply using food. Of course, I had concerns about her ability to share and her manners with other dogs where I could sum her up by saying every toy was Dare's, every toy was killed and destroyed if at all possible, and she was obsessed by herding the other dogs. So, it will be no surprise to hear that she had resource guarding issues around the cage and food in particular.

Dealing with the resource guarding of the cage was contingent on breaking the habit of taking biscuits, bones and other titbits back to her cage. And of course, I wanted her to be able to eat with the others without any problems arising.

There was another issue which was evident when Dare was out of the cage, she was unable to be still and myself and my family always described her as having 'ants in her pants'. She literally was on the move until she collapsed and lay down... usually in her cage! It was akin to a nervous energy and she tired so very quickly. Interestingly, I had hoped that with improved diet and a settled life that this rapid tiring would leave but it never has, and she will still lie down and rest on a walk even after ten or fifteen minutes.

Dare needed so very much to learn to chill and relax and lose the 'ants in her pants'. This level of activity combined with her over friendly behaviour where she was capable of jumping all over anyone and everyone made it difficult to sit and watch TV, read a book and having a coffee was simply far too dangerous for both Dare and the coffee drinkers!

I better not forget my Cockatiel who was of major interest to Dare and most definitely not in a positive way. Bob had already bore witness to the dead bird Dare killed in the garden, he couldn't believe how quickly she dispatched the poor animal. She was far more interested by the noise he made than the movement, but she certainly couldn't be trusted around him.

Rescues don't come without baggage and Dare was no exception. I guess many of the reasons for Dare's behaviour do lie in her past history however it was much more useful to listen to and observe Dare in her new environs than make suppositions about what had gone before. It was time to move on and to think of forging a happy future for Dare and fortunately for her I have a strong belief in the power of change.

6   VALUES AND PHILOSOPHY

My personal values underpin my training and I believe that the people we are influence how we undertake any job or activity in life and indeed how we relate with other humans and animals. It would be easy for me to state I am a positive dog trainer, which indeed I am, but I also bring to my training a belief in non-violence as well as a strong commitment to equality in all relationships. These beliefs bring a desire for a more equal relationship between my dogs and myself and a willingness to compromise and negotiate a mutual understanding which leads to respect for each other and trust. So, Dare and I were going to work together as a TEAM!

You might be wondering why we're discussing my beliefs and values as I did state at the outset that this wasn't a training manual, but this is so important to me, so I will briefly explain. I strongly believe that there is no point in training with a dog that you have no relationship with and I invest much of my early training be it with puppy or older rescues in building solid foundations where relationship and trust are my only focus and on which training will be more easily facilitated. My employment background as well as both graduate and post graduate education is in psychology so many years ago as an undergraduate I discovered Maslow and his hierarchy of needs.

This model originally applied to human behaviour can so easily be applied to animals too and that's what I would like to start with here. So, my plan with Dare was to improve her physiological state by providing a good diet, increasing her weight and in doing so support her bodily to cope with her life experiences. We are what we eat and the nutrients we consume are so important for appropriate weight gain and to support her stressed body and ensure good health. Despite being a vegetarian, my dogs are raw fed and I try to ensure that their raw diet is high quality and fit for human consumption with their vegetable and fruit intake being mainly organic. To her diet I added supplements such as garlic, fish oils and Ester C initially alongside a little Organic Apple cider vinegar in her water.

I wanted Dare also to feel safe and secure in her new home and environs, so I needed to ensure she was not put in the position of other dogs frightening her for example. These first two levels are basic needs which were straightforward for me to address and I intend to discuss these in forthcoming chapters.

The psychological levels are more complex, firstly of love and belonging where I wanted to work on the relationship between myself and Dare, where she learned to trust me, listen to me, but of course that's a two-way street and clearly I had to reciprocate with her and trust her, listen to her. Of course, I wasn't the only relationship that mattered, and I wanted to look at her relationship with others, both human and the other dogs in her life. From working on this I hoped she would feel both loved and a sense of belonging.

The second psychological level of esteem was clearly lacking in Dare. She was shut down and so frequently took refuge in her cage and of course with that comes 'learned helplessness'. I wanted for Dare to feel that her actions have meaning in the world and to do that I needed to ensure the foundations of the lower levels were solid. At this point the kind of training that I offered to Dare was to be so important and I am saving that for a future chapter where you'll see Dare starting to learn to think for herself and to see her actions and behaviours were valued.

The final stage of Maslow's hierarchy is Self-Actualisation, to translate this to what I expected for Dare, I wanted her to achieve all she could be, and I was positive she could be more than scared, fearful, shut down and needy. I like very much that Maslow hierarchy talks about achieving one's full potential, including creative abilities. I strongly feel that dogs' creative abilities are suppressed in mainstream dog training and that most dogs never get the opportunity to express their creative abilities and to achieve this there is a need for an approach to dog training where the dogs' actions are valued and made meaningful by the reaction of the trainer. The relationship between human and dog in most training situations is an unequal one where at worst the human demands and the dog responds. I wanted an equal partnership with my Dare where we could work cooperatively together.

So, I do call myself a behaviourist but my training moves beyond Behaviourism in that I do not solely support a stimulus – response approach to training where I provide a stimulus and my dog responds. I attribute to my dogs an inner life which I want to make part of my training and in doing so it's necessary to understand your dogs' body language and his/her personality as well as their feelings, their likes and dislikes – this is holistic, and I believe is why my dogs shine brightly through life, as well as when in the ring performing.

There was no point in training or trying to deal with any of Dare's issues relating to fear, sound, other dogs or even simply her recall issue until I could build a bond. And I needed Dare to want to interact with me on more than a basis of over friendly and displacement behaviours such as clinging to me, jumping all over me and leaning on me at every opportunity.

There were so many stories I have been told of Dare's life before I met her. One that resonates was recounted to me when I met Rachel's dad at Crufts. It highlights the fearful, clingy and needy dog that Dare was. When Rachel became very sick she lived with her Dad and step mum along with her dogs. Around firework night Rachel's screams were heard from her bedroom, when investigated Dare had spooked with the noise and had got herself on top of Rachel's head in blind panic. So many of the stories I was told made sense in terms of the Dare I had met, but looking backwards was not going to help Dare, and it was time to move forwards for the sake of Dare.

Supporting Dare to become all she could be meant looking at this hierarchy of needs from the bottom up so she was able to achieve her full potential.

I needed Dare to WANT to interact with me, to PLAY with me, to TRUST me and to LISTEN to me.

I knew this would lead to CONFIDENCE

Dare's Diary by Heather Smith

7 SHOPPING – SAFETY BUT SADLY NO SOCIALISATION

One of the lovely things about having a new companion in your life is going shopping for new bedding and accessories such as collars and leads and so forth. I especially enjoy picking colours and patterns that I think suit my dogs.

Sadly, Dare couldn't be taken along to choose, she was too scared and my single experience of taking her into a shop in the first month or so to buy and fit her for a Thundershirt was not positive. The shop we visited was not in a busy area and although I parked almost at the door by the time we reached it her ears were down. Worse still when the scary man brought the coats out she wouldn't even eat the roast beef titbits and slinked onto her belly and rolled over submissively. I can't thank the shop enough for letting me take the coats outside to try on in my van and the lovely young man for his patience and understanding.

Dare had clearly a strong history of avoidance and flight from fear and she could remove her collar in such situations, hence the tight collar I had picked her up on. Dare was an expert at getting her head out of a collar if fear drove her to flee, so alongside a new collar reflecting her new home and phone number one of the first things I bought Dare was a good fitting and secure harness of her own. I hoped she'd feel the security of wearing a harness that fitted around her body like a body wrap however we first had to deal with the flinching as it went over her head. This is not so uncommon and many dogs exhibit avoidance behaviour at things going over their heads from hands to coats! I spent time clicking and rewarding Dare for putting her head through a small hoop then an oversized collar and finally the harness – at all times allowing her to be able to move away after the click and not forcing her to remain with the collar, hoop or harness on. Simple little exercises such as this made me aware that Dare is a very quick learner, and this took no time whatsoever. So, we were ready to practice with a towel for drying off after wet walks as well as with her new coat.

I started this chapter saying that with every dog I think about the colours that suit them and I am sure Dare didn't care - this was all about me! The colour I chose for Dare was red, so she now had a name to live up to and a colour that suggests bold and brave too. She got a red harness, collar and lead, a Royal Stewart tartan coat and I even bought her red tartan blankets for her new raised bed that incidentally she took a year to use but now loves.

Dare now has a variety of colours that suit her so well and all bright and bold. These developed over time and her changes in personality which have seen her grow into a bright, bold and confident girl!

8 HEALTH & SAFETY – DIET AND THE VET

Dare was very thin and of course with having been through so much it's perhaps not surprising. She had been pretty much immersed in the varied diet that my girls eat from the word go. I have for many years fed a raw and natural diet not only from a health point of view but also in the belief that a varied diet has to be better than eating the same food day in day out and as such add value and interest to my dogs' lives – isn't variety the spice of life! I do believe that this contributes to my dogs leading happier and also longer lives. With such a stressed dog as Dare I was hoping this natural diet would help strengthen her immune system and assist her in coping with everyday life. Additionally, from the major destruction she was capable of with toys I could see she needed an outlet for chewing which the raw diet offered in the form of bones, which incidentally she has loved from day one.

All of my dogs eat together however Dare could not initially join in with mealtimes in my small kitchen. In the early days Dare found eating with the other dogs on the other side of a gate difficult and she would freeze and not eat which was often followed by growling if any of the other dogs looked in her direction and at her uneaten food. Of course, I didn't want her to be long term eating in a cage with her propensity to guard the cage as well as the food.

The other issue with food was she was greedy and fingers were at risk, so it was this issue I decided to deal with first. I am not a fan of the fashion for hand feeding your dog his or her every mouthful of food and I firmly believe that dogs should have access to food in a bowl and peace to eat it, that aside I decided on short term hand feeding. This is not an easy task with raw feeding especially given I am a vegetarian and do not like to handle meat. However, I spent most mornings and evenings sitting on the floor with Dare's rations and teaching her to take food gently. I concentrated on tasks that were calm and which focused on self-control, so I taught her to leave using her meals and also to smart lure so follow my hand with food without grabbing at me and also I started to teach a relax. At this time, I also began very informal sessions of free shaping which I will discuss later where I would reward any behaviours Dare would offer.

Very quickly the hand feeding was progressed to the food being placed into the bowl whilst I was still following the same format of working on a little training. I use the term training loosely as it was informal, and it didn't take much for Dare to scoot off to her cage – an airplane overhead (we live near a major airport), the helicopters from HMS Gannet, the neighbour playing his bagpipes and so many other triggers to her sound sensitivity and of course the triggers to her reactivity which I will also keep for a further chapter. When she left to hide in her cage I simply waited for her to come back out which in the early days could take time, so I drank another cup of coffee, checked Facebook, washed the dishes and waited and always made such a fuss of her for coming back to me. It took time and I was waiting for the fear to subside a little before the next stage which was to introduce food with the other dogs.

Of course, I also took Dare to visit my vet where she was health checked, weighed and her chip scanned and checked. She seemed healthy if thin. However, her nervous and skittish behaviour in the quiet surgery resulted in the suggestion that Dare was given Nutracalm which contains L Tryptophan, a natural enzyme which is necessary for general growth and development, producing niacin and creating serotonin in the body thus promoting a calm and relaxed mood. I would say that a difference in her behaviour was evident within a couple of months and acquaintances who I had not discussed this with commented on the change in her around the same time. Though of course it is difficult to disentangle all of the other threads of work and training I was doing with her, but I do believe the Nutracalm helped.

In the early stages and given Dare was not intended to live with me, I knew very little about her background. I did speak to a friend of Rachel's who was very helpful and of course Nicky provided me with the information I have already shared here. There were positives as well as the negatives and although Dare was clearly not good with children, fearful of men and sound sensitive by all accounts there were plusses as she was described as loving, could give a paw to the cue 'wave' and had been to an obedience class.

But of course, there were other issues, if Dare had been an easy dog she would have been quickly rehomed in the area in which she lived and she probably wouldn't have ended up in a Facebook advert.

9 WE ARE FAMILY

Dare had lived with other dogs. She had a Belgian Shepherd brother called Chaos when she was with Rachel and I am told they got on very well. In fact, I see evidence in how much Dare likes Belgian Shepherds every time we encounter one, she always looks so excited. However, the other side of this was that I was concerned about her avoidance and freezing around my dogs and a few other dogs she had met and also by the herding behaviour Nicky had described to me.

Dare was joining a household of five other free-living (not caged or kennelled) dogs and my first thoughts were of how she was going to fit in. Each of my dogs has a unique personality and it was already clear that Dare was going to find some of the dogs easier to coexist with than others.

I wasn't intent on putting Dare with them all straight away, rather I planned to introduce them all individually then in small groups. I didn't want Dare to be put in a situation where she was likely to freeze. The aim was that everyone should get along and that no, or minimum negative history should be allowed to establish between the dogs.

Her first friend amongst my dogs was Skye. I wasn't surprised at all by this as Skye had many of the same characteristics as Dare and they played in a similar style. Initially their play was like two-year-old children in parallel play, and as such when they played they would be doing the same thing but separately. Usually this involved running to and fro with balls in their mouths and I was so pleased to see the running was not herding rather it was the girls side by side and together. This quickly developed into playing with the same toys, so activities such as tugging together on the same toy or playing with the same football, and very touchingly with Dare frequently giving in to her elderly yet still nimble friend Skye. As the summer approached they both enjoyed water games such as dooking for treats in a mini paddling pool or at the local reservoir, with Dare showing no signs of guarding the food and becoming increasingly brave with water whilst also establishing another strand of confident behaviour. It gave me so much pleasure to see my lovely golden oldie Skye in her advanced years enjoying life with Dare and I am sure she passed on her confidence to Dare.

It wasn't all plain sailing and with Bonnie and Maddie there was the beginnings of bullying behaviour. Bonnie was 13 years old when Dare arrived and still the barking Bonnie she was throughout her life. Bonnie had always played and barked simultaneously and it was this that Dare reacted to. It's interesting that though Gertie plays in exactly the same way that Dare never reacted in the same way to her, perhaps it is easier to pick on the elderly, but it wasn't going to be allowed! I decided to put Gertie and Bonnie together and double the barking and play for Dare to deal with but also to let her see that Bonnie's barking was not intimidating to other dogs. I started with Dare on a lead and spent short periods of time just feeding her for watching them. The initial sessions might have been no more than a minute and we worked up over weeks to longer periods, before moving on to calling Bonnie and Gertie for a treat too. How easy life was for me here as neither Bonnie or Gertie are very foody and have always preferred to play. It wasn't too long before all three were eating together initially at a little distance as I stretched my arms out then closer and closer as I could see Dare look happy and relaxed with the situation. I didn't release Dare to immediately play as I knew that herding Bonnie and Gertie would be paramount in her mind after all she didn't really know how to play in the way that these two play with such gusto, bouncing, barking, lots of use of paws and a very in your face and full on manner. I spent time with the three of them asking for tricks initially all doing the same activity – which was very limited as Dare's repertoire was sit, down, touch (a hand target) and wave – then introducing a little turn taking where one did a trick and the others watched, though I have to say Dare was the focus of most of the tricks due to her inability to be still. Dare surrounded herself with activity so she didn't have to think about the world, she still had ants in her pants and this was to be the case for some time to come! As her focus on me grew and her interest in the games of Bonnie and Gertie declined she was happy to interact without herding and the potential for nipping that went with this. The kind of play that developed between this trio was primarily running together especially later on when outdoors and Dare was allowed off lead. Dare was always polite with the older Bonnie even after her stroke when vulnerability could have lent itself to bullying behaviour and she is to this day always very submissive with Gertie.

The situation with Maddie was more complex as she is also a fearful dog. Two fearful dogs are generally not a good combination and it is the relationship between these two that has taken me the longest to resolve and which has on occasion broken down. There are similarities between these two dogs, both are clingy and want to be with me and have a strong desire to please however there are big differences too. Maddie is not a fighter and is really quite cowardly around other dogs, she always gives in and relinquishes the toys because her focus is totally on me. The sentence I speak to Maddie most is 'Be a Dog' by which she understands that interaction with me is over and it is time to focus on her canine friends and activities. Dare is more of a 'street kid' and her freezing was my biggest worry, and I was right to be worried. I had several small incidents with these two and then one around two years later but each of these incidents had the potential to be very serious. With every one of the small incidents it was a blessing that Maddie was no fighter as Dare really would have kept a fight going that was totally one sided, as Maddie simply stood still. This is a tremendously difficult situation to deal with as it has the potential to be so rewarding for the aggressor. So much work was done with every tool and strategy in my toolbox of tricks to foster a relationship where these two could get along. I spent time working with one while the other watched with the safety of my garden fence separating them and then removing the fence where I had friends who were willing to hold one at a time. I rewarded both as equally as possible with the difficulty that Dare just could not be still and Maddie eyed her if she was too aroused. So initially the focus was on calm games at home and activities such as swimming or treading water at the beach when outdoors with Dare on lead of course. Over time I was able to increase their arousal by upping the excitement of the play using chuckit stick and ball for example and when needed increasing the distance between them to keep them self-controlled and not lunging in Dare's case or barking in Maddie's case. It took till around just short of six months before I considered feeding them together and at that point I felt they both looked relaxed. I would say the relationship between Dare and Maddie is one of ignoring each other but without the arousal of freezing that can lead to a fight situation. They can eat together, chew bones in the same room, walk the same walk but they don't really interact together in play. In the four and a half years they have been together there has been one other incident. It took place whilst out walking with a few dogs we know plus two new dogs which suggest context and arousal may have played a part, and they were all swimming for a few balls. I saw Dare freeze (which hadn't happened in so long) and though Maddie was on the other side of the group of around ten dogs, she went straight for Maddie and though Maddie didn't retaliate I know Dare would have continued if I hadn't intervened. They were immediately separated and I returned to the basics of training them back together the next day. I have to say it was like a blip, a slip of normal behaviour and there has been no repetition of this. I guess for dogs it's the same as for humans and as such we can't like everyone, but we can learn to live respectfully together.

I did worry about Dare with Dinky, my Bichon Frise but this worry was misguided. My initial concern was over a problem Dinky had at the time with her skin whereby she scratched till she squeaked, and of course I had seen Dare's behaviour around things that squeaked. There were the balls and toys which she could destroy in no time at all, my pet Cocktail was under guard from her snapping at the cage especially when he was noisy and there was an incident where she killed a wild bird in my garden in front of my partner Bob's eyes – he couldn't believe she had done it! However, the confident and bossy, Dinky was a firm friend very early on. It was no time before they played together in their very mouthy style, they would relax and sleep on the couch next to each other and Dare always gave way to Dinky so whether it was a toy or food if Dinky wanted it Dare let her have it. This pair have never had a cross word and when they play it is all about mouthing. They are a joy to watch together with Dare playing the role of a gentle giant and Dinky as her feisty little friend!

Such was the start of Dare's integration and from this point I moved on to putting them all together in a play situation such as I have described above. The theory is if they are happy and behaving at home then in the great big world when we venture out all will be well!

10 HOUSEKEEPING

As well as working on relationships between the girls, there were a variety of housekeeping issues that needed urgently addressed.

If Dare couldn't cope with the increasing list of sound sensitivities then it was going to be difficult to get her to be relaxed at home and of course exercised as she was unable to walk in a straight line for any length of time. Walks were proving very difficult as she scooted here and there, lunged in fear and as such walks were not enjoyable for Dare, nor for myself if this was to continue. My arms felt like they were popping out of their sockets on a walk and whilst this continued I was going to be unable to walk all my dogs together. The joy of walking dogs was no joy in the early stages with Dare and she couldn't be let off lead because of the herding behaviour and her inability to listen whilst I suspected her recall was not very solid outdoors. Her need for exercise was obvious and I believe all dogs need opportunities for exercise both on and off lead daily. In total my girls enjoy around three hours a day mostly free running exercise and in the early stages Dare didn't get nearly this amount. This was a priority which I am going to deal with in a later chapter but for the meantime it worried me but coping at home was a huge priority.

Sound sensitivity was a major barrier to Dare being able to live life and to learn and more importantly to her coping at home. She wasn't my first sound sensitive dog and it's a common problem in Bearded Collies as well as in other breeds. My first Beardie managed to dig up tiles in the bathroom floor and was so fearful of cars on wet roads and fireworks, so I had certainly been here before with my own dogs as well as others dogs!

I made a list of triggers to Dare's sound sensitivity at home and divided them into outside in the garden and indoors and then prioritised them.

With outdoors the major fear factor was the planes taking off from Prestwick Airport which go over our home and the helicopters from HMS Gannet which were less regular. Windy weather was a problem both in the big outdoor world but also in my garden where some of the sounds like the garage roof were obvious triggers, but other sounds were not obvious to me but clearly were relevant to Dare. Indoors she didn't like certain noises on the radio or on television often noises from the real world such as banging, bagpipes, children playing. The lists were lengthy and Dare's reactions the same – usually flight to the cage and occasionally if I was sitting watching TV she'd jump onto me no matter what I was doing usually trying to get behind me where she felt safe. Sound sensitivity is such a big issue it deserves a chapter of its own, but I have to mention it here as it was such a big part of Dare's home life but so intrinsically part of the many issues Dare had that I can't separate it from the other issues. At times it felt like a mountain I could never climb and conquer and at the root of so many other issues so it had to be addressed.

It's probably no surprise that Dare felt safe in her cage, it's likely that she lived in a cage a great deal of the time at Wiccaweys prior to her rescue by Rachel. But there is no point in harking back to Dare's past and looking for an explanation as I could never be sure and despite suspicions, we both had to move on. Of course, that Dare guarded her cage was no surprise. I've already mentioned her food guarding behaviour out with the cage and when given a bone to chew on it was far from unknown from her to take it, run to her cage and guard it. I was still working on the growling around food in June 2014 and as I have said I was feeding her mostly out with the cage where I could easily take bones from her, however within the cage I was wary as she was still so defensive so I didn't push her till I could gain her confidence in me. One other issue with the cage was avoiding her being put in a situation where any of the others tried to get in with her especially if she was in their due to a fear reaction and with this I knew I had to be vigilant and of course the flight path to the cage was littered with other dogs and she would snap if they were in her way. I maintained vigilance around this situation and my other dogs were well behaved and left Dare to her flight and cage and perhaps due to these factors there were never any issues. I have to say that Dare really isn't a bad dog, her intentions were self-preservation rather than destruction and it's my belief that that too played an enormous role in this situation being resolved. It's so often the case that it's not the interventions we make that change a situation and it's human arrogance that we feel the need to believe we fix things when the reality is so different. So, I have to tell you about a morning in September 2014 when I was sitting in the kitchen keeping up with the news with a coffee and as usual one eye on the girls. Dare had come scooting in from outside and I registered the sound of an airplane overhead. I was watching her in the back of the cage as the beardies got up and went outside, I was wondering whether they were leaving her in peace on her own, perhaps even giving her space when heart in hand I saw Dinky had headed into the cage with Dare and I saw Dare look away from her, avoid her and remain very still. I confess to the desire to interfere, but I didn't and what transpired says so much about their blossoming relationship and the help one dog can give another. Dinky lay down, Dare followed suit and I watched the two of them relax together. I've no idea how long I watched for, but it was Dinky who then got up, licked Dare around her face and although Dare didn't react other than to let the licking continue she raised her head and looked relaxed with the situation. Again, it was Dinky who initiated activity by leaving the cage, picking up a toy and watching Dare, who chose to join her. They played initially with the little squeaky soft toy and taking turns with Dinky grumbling as she played and tossing it and Dare getting a brief game of kill it, then the toy was discarded they got down to playing with each other. They play with lots of mouthing and with Dinky doing the rough and tumble and climbing all over Dare. Dare has always been so gentle with Dinky, so self-controlled even in fearful situations.

One issue that was a priority to sort was running the fence between my neighbour and our house, which was more pronounced when the children were playing. It was clear this was about the children as she only was interested in one neighbour, my other neighbour being elderly and Dare having quickly made friends with her. Concerns had been raised about Dare with children and I've already said that her chasing went as far as being described as 'nappy nipping' and my neighbour has a large family of active young children. Spring weather was upon us as Dare arrived here so the children were often out playing in their garden and often the number of children multiplied as their friends joined them. It was clear that the sound of the children playing and the noise of their play was enough to trigger her interest and the fence chasing started with this. Dare's life was being severely curtailed by being kept on lead, but it was my first port of call and I did much work with her on lead and feeding her for not chasing, playing with her for tricks given but dogs are aware when they are on lead and off lead even with loose lead handling which I always use and advocate. I knew her listening skills would suffer if she started fence chasing but I wanted her off lead, so I set up a fence within the garden boundary fence to increase the distance between Dare and the children – a no man's land, or more specifically a no-Dare land. I had several shots at this till I got the distance right where she didn't want to chase the new fence and I used lots of energetic games she enjoyed such as football and tagged on listening skills such as her ever increasing repertoire of tricks before playing again though I concentrated a lot on recall and play for the obvious reason that I wanted to be able to recall her from the fence or children. And you may be asking why arousing games, well in brief I do believe having a good recall is contingent on a dog wanting to play with you and food is unlikely to cut it! I even went as far as recruiting the other dogs that I knew liked to lie in the shade of the hedge especially Gertie and Skye so that when I had a much-needed rest from the energetic games she could watch them, and I hoped see their total disinterest in the children. This issue was one of the easier ones to resolve as I simply moved her barrier fence closer to the garden fence then removed it totally. Children were an issue in other ways which I will return to but meantime we had made a huge step forward to prepare Dare for children in the real world and I have my neighbours' children to thank for this. The relationship between Dare and our youngest neighbour, a preschool aged little boy became ever so sweet.

At the time my neighbours had no dogs but this youngest child really liked watching the girls and speaking to them through our fence. Whilst hanging out washing I was listening to him speaking to the dogs and could see none of the dogs were bothering, but I was keeping an eye on Dare who was very interested in him and I was ready to intervene if she was naughty. I then saw firstly what I believe was a sandwich come through the hedge which was promptly eaten, it was quickly followed by an apple which Dare proceeded to play with as if it were a ball to the child's accompanying laughter! Feeding Dare through the hedge became quite a regular occurrence!

Of course, we have visitors to our house and women were never an issue for Dare, she was always friendly and welcoming with them, and though I had been told Dare wasn't good with men initially I didn't see any evidence of this. Dare had been absolutely fine with Michelle's husband and his friends as well as with my partner and son and their friends. We even had delivery men drop off parcels and so forth and she didn't bat an eyelid nor was the postman of any interest at all.

What a lovely note to move on from …… well, we shall see!

11 FIRST THINGS FIRST – PLAY AND BONDING

Of course, it's easy to focus on the negative issues which required addressing, but there were plenty positives too and of primary importance was her desire to be with me and to please me (most of the time!). I couldn't have asked for a better base from which to work from. So, my first objective was to build a bond with Dare which was not based solely on her need of me, and I knew this would be to some extent easy, little could I have predicted how strong her trust would come to be.

There are always plenty toys in our home so there had been so many opportunities for Dare to play with different kinds of toys – soft, hard, noisy, rubber, plastic, furry, varied shapes and so on! I had been told Dare liked a ball and plastic hoops, and I made sure she had both of these. Dare loved to play and was certainly keen on balls of all kinds – she really enjoyed the chasing and catching involved in these games. However, I had found she really liked toys that made a sound especially squeaky type, soft toys which she enjoyed chasing, shaking, catching and of course killing (destuffing or picking at the fur!). I have always given my Beardies (a breed where there is sound sensitivity) noisy toys in an attempt to get them used to unexpected and unusual sounds, buying many children's toys as these offer all kinds of noise. So, I added so many new noisy toys to the toy baskets and frequently Gertie showed Dare what was 'expected'.

So, it was easy to predict the toys she'd play with from the toy baskets and around our home, but her repertoire of choice was growing! That said she still didn't play with such strength in that if there was a noise she wouldn't take flight, but I knew that this was clearly to be the route to bonding and getting to know Dare. From an established relationship so much can be achieved, and we needed this badly, so that I was worth listening to in Dare's eyes. I needed to become part of her games.

All training with my dogs is based on mutual respect and establishing a partnership. An ethological approach to training stemming from understanding one's dog and tailoring training to suit that dog is something I've attempted with all my hairy companions. This is a two-way street and for my part I did my level best to read Dare's body language and act contingently on what she was saying to me. If there were signs of stress or anxiety and if Dare chose to go chill in her cage then Dare had to be listened to even if this was the time I had set aside to spend with her, and even if this was to be the only time I had available that day. She was never on a lead for any of these sessions as it was her choice to remain with me that was what mattered, and inevitably there were days when she would shoot off during play and return almost straight away and other days where she obviously felt it was too much and we did very little. As such how I handled Dare and behaved with her was vitally important, and her choices were paramount. There was no one size fits all training programme, in fact intuition and understanding was to be the order of the day and my hope was that Dare would make the choice to be with me.

I was quietly confident that at some point the desire to play and the intrinsic enjoyment of play would become paramount in Dare and that fear and flight would be less and less likely. In tipping this seesaw towards the direction of play as opposed to the side of fear and flight, I knew Dare's bond with me would grow as would her confidence and ability to cope with life.

I like to play with my puppies or new dogs initially sitting with them at their level, as opposed to towering over them. This was initially very difficult with Dare as she couldn't help herself from leaning on me and mobbing me to the extent that I could barely remain sitting. This over-needy and clingy behaviour highlighted that she was not coping in life independently however I had no intention of pushing her off, so I started our games sitting in a chair. Of course this didn't mean she never mobbed me but it was far less likely..... except of course when triggered by a fear response.

So whilst I was sitting in my chair Dare was very happy to play with me as she had clearly learned to tug strongly on toys and though as I had observed from her routing of the toy boxes soft toys were her favourites she was happy to tug on more or less anything I presented her with. Of course not all toys have the same value and early on I was constantly checking out favourites which we could use in training. These varied over time and sometimes with the introduction of something new, and I reacted and responded to Dare's choices and preferences.

So, I really did start from a fantastic position with a dog that already played, and this allowed me to take this play onto the periphery of fear zones. I knew that should we get too close to anything that Dare feared she would take flight, so I can't stress strongly enough that it was out with her fear zone where we started our play. Here, she could cope sufficiently and at no point did I deliberately flood her with fear by putting her into a situation where she could not cope. Early on we played in a variety of environments both at home and in the real world. At home we played around the television as there were certain things she didn't enjoy as much as I did. I recorded these programmes and in one instance advert and allowed them to run whilst playing initially in the next room and then latterly near the television itself. In the real world one of Dare's fears was the sound of the wind in the trees on the edge of the woods (I often wonder if she equated this with the wind in the wooden barns in the rescue centre she had been in prior to being rescued by Rachel and this was one of the saddest things I feel I have dealt with, as my dogs all just love walks in the woods as indeed you would expect a dog to). I knew from day one Dare feared the trains on railway lines and this was one of the early things I worked on as several of our regular walks skirt these locations. Working on proximity and getting closer to her target fear whilst using play was so successful in this case that I was finally able to take Dare on the train to the next town in just over a year and this involved so many other fear factors such as all the new noises and the different environment of the train stations not to mention the male ticket conductor. To say I was proud of Dare is a gross understatement as she took it in her stride and the reward at the next station of a walk on the beach was much appreciated and of course by this time she was also able to be off lead in the context of the beach. Later on I was able to take play into venues at shows we'd be attending which became the basis for so much more!

The focus of these early session was always on the play, I knew from playing at home that it was relatively easy to get Dare to leave a toy she was playing with, though again I should say that this was dependent on the toy itself and it took time before she was able to leave the noisier toys she really loved! And I was spending lots of time rather than focusing on Dare leaving and dropping the toy, with me letting go of the toy whilst we were tugging together to see if she would reengage with me by returning with the toy. This happened so very quickly and I often ended these sessions with time spent cuddling with Dare thus emphasising that play was all about us being together. Of course Dare loved this as she has always enjoyed expressing herself with physical contact and affection and I have to admit to being rather partial to Dare's cuddles myself!

I play train with all my dogs and use it in behavioural consultations as well as in puppy classes. I would strongly advocate play as building a better bond between handler and dog as it provides the building blocks for any future training and behaviour. More importantly it also reduces dependence on luring with food which brings with it, if not carefully used problems associated with the food becoming the cue to behaviour as well as issues around a lack of body awareness and listening skills. These were all skills I wanted Dare to develop.

Play is not solely about tugging on a toy however, and that is evident if you observe dogs playing amongst themselves where they spend time in a variety of activities. My girls play together without the assistance of a toy they enjoy running together, they roll around mouthing and pawing at each other, they lie down after all of their games and rest together. So much of this is tactile and sometimes vocal. Dare had work to do in the early days to develop her relationships with some of her canine sisters and move away from freezing and fear based response to other dogs especially in smaller spaces, but I could see she had these skills and wanted to use these in her play with me.

Now I am very aware that humans are not dogs but we can to some extent simulate some of these activities with our dogs and indeed I believe we do. We run with our dogs at agility and in cani fit, we spend time cuddling our dogs and feel the benefits of this in terms of proven effects on our health and wellbeing. All of this contributes to the relationship we have together.

I've often referred to the cuddle and tactile time I spend with my dogs as 'Bonding Time', indeed I have been running classes on Play and Bonding for six years now, and so encouraging others to do so too! Dare was a huge fan of this time and enjoyed leaning on me rolling around on the floor with me moving under my legs and arms and body on the floor and at the end of a session curling up on the couch. Sometimes she was over the top and couldn't contain herself from jumping all over me at which point I would introduce food to interrupt this behaviour and it was usually sufficient to calm her down. She very rarely left this type of play to escape to the cage, she clearly felt safe and loved it too much.

Over many years and from experience I've learnt that it's not simply good enough to have a dog hyped and overexcited hanging on the end of a tuggy in order for the dog to listen and work for you. Indeed, this kind of play is not suited to all dogs anyway and in colloquial terms over arousal can lead to the dogs' mind being blown which is counterproductive as the dog loses the ability to listen and hear what you are saying. That aside there are dogs who love it and Dare is one of these dogs.

It was relatively simple to teach Dare a 'leave' cue by playing swapsies with her where I exchanged one game for another, initially offering a like for like exchange by having toys of the same value but then by playing with games such as can you swap for something of a lesser value – don't forget I had been observing her favourite toys, partly with this in mind. If that was difficult for her then I would offer something of a higher value for a few repetitions then return to the more challenging swaps. It wasn't long before I could add the cue 'leave' and start to apply it out with the swapping games. The same cue was added to other games such as food leaving activities, so it was quickly becoming a concept of move away when you hear the word 'leave'. I have to tell you about one of Dare's favourite food leaving games which we usually play when I make toast. It highlights the moving away she does when she hears that cue. I normally cut up a few little squares of toast and line these along the edge of the kitchen worktop and there is normally a lot of excitement about this as it's a game for all the girls together, once they have learnt to leave. I wait for the excitement and interest in the toast to rise and then on leave they all move away, walking backwards. It's at that point I mark the behaviour with a click or click word and they get the toast.

However, I knew that I needed to build in impulse control which involves more than simply a 'leave' cue on a tuggy or with food. What I worked on with Dare was learning to come down from play into calm and be able to recommence play again. And I felt this was possible at the time her fear responses were less likely to interfere with play, in short when she stopped running away whenever she heard something! So new games commenced of play followed by a statue like pose from Dare, which in the early days were simple behaviours such as sit, down or stand but over time we added in behaviours from Dare's growing repertoire. And given Dare's difficulty standing still they had to be brief moments of static – don't forget the standing joke with Dare from her family and friends was that she had 'ants in her pants'!

There was another calming exercise I worked on with Dare where I spent time teaching her a chill /relax pose. This is a useful thing to teach not only from the point of view of relaxing but for grooming, examining your dog and so on. I have been interested in this since doing a canine massage course many years ago and I do believe in the benefits of this for all my dogs who volunteer for a massage regularly. Initially massage with Dare was impossible, as I have already said I couldn't sit on the floor with her without being mobbed, she couldn't stay still for very long and her desire to lean on me and jump all over me was far from helpful. I decided to teach her to do the relaxing but I started with a quandary – her down was rigid and tense and often resulted in her rolling over into a fearful and submissive pose. Looking at her eyes in these positions told me she was far from happy. I dropped the clicker from my training with this as it was too arousing and with bagfuls of treats sat on the floor with her rewarding any micro behaviour that meant she moved closer to lying flat on the floor. By rewarding small steps, it wasn't long before Dare was offering a complete lay flat on her side especially on her left side though we did work on both sides! I am going to talk about shaping in a future chapter so will return to this but at no point did I lure her behaviour rather I rewarded what she did herself ...... Dare's choice was paramount! From this fabulous achievement Dare has now moved on to learn to relax her whole body, and allow her head, body and feet to be lifted as a dead weight and I would suggest that she's learned through this to relax tense muscles but also to trust me.

Play wasn't all about me though and I have already mentioned her play with my dogs and other dogs she had met. With my dogs she found it much easier to play with the more naturally confident dogs. No surprise that her first playmate was my elderly, Skye who was the dog dare reminded me of in looks in her rehome me advert. It turned out they were similar in other ways such as they both played in a primitive way using their mouths, rolling around a lot like a pair of wrestlers. Skye was the best playmate for Dare as in situations where Dare wanted to bolt or worse still froze Skye was bombproof. It's established that dogs fall into different play types and indeed straddle these, so it makes sense that some combinations are more successful than others and Dare's preferences were quickly obvious in that she liked to play with those with a similar style of play such as Skye, Dinky and later on Google. She didn't really get Bonnie and Gertie's barking, bouncing and paw-based play, though Gertie and Dare's relationship serves to illustrate that context can make such a difference as outdoors and off lead these two love running and tugging together. And let's not forget personality is important and Dare prefers confident dogs.

I wanted Dare's explorative play to be developed too so that her confidence would grow. I provided interactive toys, games such as dooking for treats in a child's swimming pool or in the local reservoir and scent games. These were precursors to starting shaping and learning for herself. I wanted Dare to appreciate that her actions in the world had meaning – in many ways Dare showed glimpses learned helplessness from the cage bound behaviour to the inability to offer behaviour where her actions were so often contingent on myself or worse still her fear-based responses.

Play and bonding was our starting point for so much and were the beginnings of Dare moving from helpless learner following instructions, being shown and lured to active learner participating in our sessions together and making behaviour choices.

Early photos are very rare

Dare and Skye -early best friends

March 2014 - Happy times playing with her ball

June 2014 – No walk today

June 2014 – Thugging Michelle

Maddie and Dare learn to co-exist

June 2014 From L to Right, Dare, Jaxon, Dinky, Maddie, Bonnie, Skye and Gertie

Dare looking away as usual

Dare still avoiding looking, this time with Bonnie

May 2014 – Still on lead at the scary Windfarm

Out and about with Michelle and the Bichons

Taking play to different places

Skye and Dare and some park training

Dare having a shaping session after a swim, and likely followed by a rewarding swim too

Bandanas – one of many!   Supergirl

Luna – fear gives way to friendship   Another new Friend, Flurry   Puppy Google and Bob

Dare's first Routine – Saddle Up (Photo by Alan Brown)   Above, the Gypsy Routine at Crufts and also below left, complete with fancy footwork.(Photos Demelza van der Lans) (Below Right, Dare's Crufts companions

Dare, finalist in the HTM at the Open European Championships in Belgium 2017 (pictures by Dagmar Richter

Dare and her fellow Team Scotland members
From top Left, Penny Mansfield's Australian Shepherds,
Roxy and Flurry, Michelle Porter's Luna, Dare, Marie
Docherty's WSD, Erin, my Dinky and Gertie

Filming at Scottish Television

12 THE REAL WORLD

Dogs generally like to go on walks, but this was not always the case for Dare. In the first year there were days when the lady wasn't for moving and Dare remained in her cage, sometimes at home but usually in my van while I reluctantly left her to walk the others.

Of course, I can be both persuasive and patient so Dare often joined us on a walk. In the early days she was always on a lead or a long line and she really enjoyed sniffing and exploring her world. Many of our walks were quiet and you would expect that in such situations she wouldn't experience too many worries. One of the saddest and most distressing things I experienced was Dare's fear of the wind in the woods on a wild and blowy day. Her radar ears would go back, she would shoot around on the end of her lead, she was so scared she didn't hear me or want to eat any tasty treats and if she were not on a lead she would most certainly have bolted away. Of course, Scottish weather can be unpredictable and we could start a walk on a calm day but the wind could rise as we walked so our return to my van could be very rapid and involve my being yanked and pulled this way and that. And of course, Dare would be so desperate to get into her cage she could barely wait for the van door to be opened, let alone her cage door. It was so distressing to see her at the back of the cage curled up very small, often shaking and so very shut down.

From the wind in the trees to the wind and high waves at the beach which Dare also feared. Yet the beach was probably the outdoors place that Dare loved most and it was one of the first places I was able to let her off lead. Prior to that on her long line it was plain to see that she could cope even on the most blustery of days when the kite surfers were surfing the waves with the proviso that a distance was maintained and there were plenty of games and activities for her to engage in. She really learnt very rapidly that we could go close to the waves and the scary kites that fly overhead on a windy day, and that there was no need to be frightened and take flight.

I can clearly recall the day I let Dare off lead on the beach. With my heart in my hands and some Beardies to lend Dare support, I unclipped the lead fed her a whole lot of roast beef and off she went. I have often talked about the joy of my dogs running and the need that dogs have to run free and seeing Dare confidently enjoy herself still brings tears to my eyes. I can only imagine that Dare felt amazing and so liberated from her worries and of course we kept returning to the beach almost daily so she could run free and happy.

However, life is rarely without setbacks and around a fortnight after I'd started to let Dare off lead we visited a different local beach. All was going so very well until two lively young Collies approached us, and Dare seemed to lose the power of hearing. Off she went running with them and then there was a return to the herding behaviour I had worked so hard to stop around my own dogs. There was no point in shouting at her to come back and the Collies owner couldn't get her dogs back either, eventually an exhausted Dare scooted back to me and I quietly popped her back on the lead. It's often hard not to be disappointed but the plus was that she returned, and the down side was that I had more work to do with this girl around high energy, exciting dogs!

My work takes me out and about to various places and my dogs come with me so there were plenty of different experiences for Dare to encounter. In terms of socialisation you would think this would be a huge positive and it certainly allowed me to quickly add to Dare's list of fears. There were times when Dare was immersed in the feared situation simply because it happened and we would have no control of the situation such as when the dreaded airplanes went overhead. I did not wish Dare to be flooded with fear but with these experiences there was no avoiding them.

Fortunately, there were plenty of visits where I was more able to control the fear factors. Our trips to local towns using different times of the day to experience the quieter hours in the early morning and later on in the afternoon then building up to the busier lunch times and the end of the school day. We visited Troon, my home town on many occasions. I'd park in the car park and head to the busier streets with the shops then reward Dare with a run on the beach before retracing our steps back to the car park. I'd always be vigilant to potential fear factors such as the lorries making deliveries with their noisy lift and ramps and at such points we could cross the road or spend a little time walking towards it and away just to check for a reaction and also to allow Dare to watch. Wherever we walked I tried to pick areas where I was familiar with the kind of noises and other fear factors we might meet and of utmost importance, where I knew potential escape routes!

It was certainly not always a pretty sight to see me walking Dare if she was in a fearful state and I was always thankful she never managed to get the harness off, in the same way I knew she could get a collar off!

There were other issues in the real world which we'll return to later but for the meantime I did what so many people with new dogs do ..... I took her to school!

13 BACK TO SCHOOL

Dog training classes are not for everyone and they are not for every dog straight away. Dare was one of those dogs who needed time to settle and with whom I hoped to form a bond prior to taking her into a class environment. Of course, I had the luxury of using my own classes as a drop-in resource and also was I fortunate to have a friend willing to help with Dare. As such from the very day of Dare's new home rejection she was welcomed into my class for no more than five minutes in the capable and sympathetic hands of Michelle.

I can clearly recall that first visit to one of my classes. She scrambled up the stairs as she was none too keen on the noise of her paws on the metal steps, she was taking in the whole environment which was understandable, but her fear of the situation resulted in her lowering her body and her antennae ears going back and then her appeasing behaviour and leaning all over anyone who spoke to her. That first trip could have been much worse, but it was telling in that she was far from comfortable in a class and in this new environment setting.

Dare had been to training classes with Rachel, so I was hopeful that she would settle. I had several classes where Dare was able to pop in and visit with Michelle for just a few minutes. My classes are always small in numbers as I don't like to intake more than six dogs at a time. This allows for a quiet learning environment for dogs and handlers and would make for an easier visit for Dare too.

Dare found it very difficult particularly in my Irvine classes where further noise sensitivities were evident such as the garage doors closing in the next building and the wind on shutter doors. At East Kilbride I have noted that even by August when she had been visiting the class for four months she found noises to worry her such as a flapping polystyrene roof tile. Of course, Michelle and I had a plan, so we used quiet class time to bring Dare in often when the dogs were working on activities such as chilling and relaxing, we knew the times the garage closed for the night so avoided such times and of course there was the plan for what Dare would be doing as she visited. This plan would include nothing too static in the early stages as Dare found that impossible even when she was not in a stressed state, she would only take part in activities she loved to do, she would eat the highest value titbits and play with her favourite toys and of course in the early days she was just in and out. So, as you'll have gathered she certainly wasn't taking part in the class curriculum.

I am fortunate to have my own class to have been able to do this, but the sad truth was in the early days she was far keener to get out of the class and into the van and her cage, and this was despite Michelle's best efforts to end the visit on a positive note. We did take advantage of the light nights throughout that first summer with Dare to walk with some of the dogs in the class and get Dare meeting people. All of this made for a very rewarding follow up to less than five minutes in class and Dare really enjoyed it.

Over time, Michelle's life was easier, Dare's desire to get into the class became enthusiastic and it was far less likely that she wished to leave! It was becoming apparent that more than most dogs I've known, if you could ensure a positive experience in a given environment Dare's ability to cope in that environment in subsequent visits was incredible and quick to improve. Dare's freezing and fear became less, and she started to participate in the class activities. Dare needed an active and busy class and my Trick class was ideal for her and in Michelle's company she leant lots of tricks. Even two years later I was noting in Dare's little diary that the most difficult thing for Dare is staying still or learning very static behaviours such as stays so as you can see it was a long journey!

Isn't it always the case that just when things appear more settled then something would happen to result in a step backwards- life is rarely a journey from A to B without rerouting along the way! There was a night at Irvine through Dare's first summer where she was so very unsettled and desperate to get out of the class. Neither Michelle nor I could see what was bothering her, but she was allowed out and of course you can imagine my feeling of disappointment in the situation as I couldn't bring an explanation to bear on what had happened when things had been going so very well. By the start of my second class there was thunder and lightning which was clearly the explanation as Dare had already showed fear at home under these weather conditions. Of course, what I did see was that this girl was a fighter- she was starting to recover faster, not hold on to her fear associations and she was coping. I have on many occasions been disappointed in myself for not understanding or being able to pick up on what Dare was telling me, but I have never been disappointed in Dare. I know she does not want to be in such a state and it is not her fault if she should feel fearful but more than anything I really have never met another dog with such an ability to overcome her fears – she really is well named!

We all want to stay in our comfort zones and of course I didn't want to push Dare too soon, but I was asking myself was it time to attend a class where we could take part together. As grateful as I was to Michelle I wanted to be able to work with my own dog! By Autumn of her first year with me, Dare looked more settled and comfortable at home as well as in the environments I was exposing her to. I was also starting to feel we had the beginnings of a relationship of trust where in most situations Dare listened to me.

It's important that the class you attend with your dog is one you will be comfortable in and where you both trust and have confidence in the trainer. So, the class I picked was Linda Rutherford's obedience class and we attended alongside Michelle and her new Bearded Collie puppy Luna. Even as a puppy Luna was a very confident dog and Dare enjoyed playing with her, so I felt this might help to settle her.

Linda is a very experienced trainer who reads and understands dogs well and her class is quiet, well run and organised but Dare's first night wasn't easy. I wasn't expecting it would be to be honest as it was another new environment and new environments were never easy in the early days. I couldn't identify sound sensitivity however she was clearly wary and attempting to revert to hiding behind chairs and my legs where she could.

The first night brought a new concern to light. There was a man in the class who Dare was terrified of to the point where she was lunging and vocalising at him. I had been told Dare didn't like men, but she had met plenty men both at home and out with and had shown no interest in them, quite the contrary she'd been her usual friendly self, if not her over friendly self on occasion! True to form Dare was quick to recover with this particular man who was kind enough to spend time encouraging her forward to take titbits from him under Linda's supervision. But I was on alert now and it quickly became apparent that it was a physical build and possibly even a voice type that Dare did not like.

I continued attending Linda's classes where Dare blossomed. Rather predictably she enjoyed the heelwork sessions and anything around movement but struggled with stays or wait for recall, so I never left her for any length of time or indeed increased much distance between her and myself. There would always be another day when we could work on these things when she was more confident.

Training with someone who clearly cares for and has your dog's best interests at heart was just what Dare needed and we have a lot to thank Linda for. Linda still sees Dare and has contributed this …

'When I first met Dare she was a very confused and insecure little dog, to the point when she would have nipped out of fear and not knowing who to trust or who was fully on her side. I have watched Dare flourish through the years in Heather's sympathetic hands, never pushing her beyond her limitations and always encouraging her every step of the way. She's now a happy, confident little dog because Heather had it in her to give her the chance she so needed. I applaud Heather for giving her the chance she so longed for and never judging her while helping her every step of the way. If everyone had it in them to rescue a scared, confused little dog the world would be a brighter place'

Linda Rutherford, three times Crufts Obedience winner

14 LEARNING TO LEARN

There is nothing more empowering than knowing that your actions in the world are meaningful and valued - It is this that I wanted Dare to experience. What I knew was that if Dare could feel and achieve this that her confidence would grow and she would become a more independent and less clingy personality. It would free her to express herself in different ways and become an active learner.

It was my belief that Dare was shut down in the early days when she feared life out with her cage and it isn't an exaggeration to describe her behaviour as that of 'learned helplessness'. I wanted to move Dare on from this state of helpless learner following instructions, being shown and lured by food and transform her into an active learner making behaviour choices in our sessions together.

My method of choice was free shaping, and it is an approach to training I have used with so many of my dogs, having started in the 1980's as a student. I had always been interested in psychology, this interest starting when I was a student teacher and has continued and grown through my career. I love the learning through exploration and the fine tuning of this through the use of verbal feedback, I usually say 'yes' or via a click with a clicker. And more than anything I love the creativity it fosters, and I have been privileged to live with so many creative companions.

These early shaping sessions were very brief, perhaps only 20 rapid clicks and titbits and focused onto a box. Dare offered very little, she either sat still or jumped all over me or worse still ran away to her cage. And my usual tack with a young or beginner dog of sitting on the floor was definitely not possible as nothing happened other than my being jumped on! When she did offer something, it was the same thing repeatedly and usually it involved variations of her left paw 'wave' that she had clearly learnt before she came to live with me. Micro behaviours or movements were very much the order of the day where I clicked and rewarded smallest of movements and shifts in body weight and slowly but surely Dare started to get the idea of this game.

Shaping allows you to discover a lot about your dogs' style of learning and Dare's style was rigid. Once a behaviour was established it was repeated a lot and each session started to repeat the previous session. I tried a variety of little tricks of my own to try to interrupt her repetition, but she was so internally focused on her own rigid behaviour that external changes to her environment made no difference at all!

I had Dare watch the sessions with the other girls. She must have watched Gertie, who is the most creative learner I have ever known and wondered what she was all about. Gertie was the opposite of Dare, she offers so many different things it is hard to keep up with her! I firmly believe that dogs learn by watching so I was hoping that some of Gertie's creativity would rub off on her!

What I do know is that there is no right and wrong – Gertie's creative variations often make it difficult to turn her offered behaviours into behaviours on cue due to the lack of repetition however Dare's more repetitive style allowed me to rapidly name her behaviours.

To move Dare on and foster some creativity I needed to try and break the rigidity of these sessions. She had already started to offer some of the more established behaviours which now had a cue (or command) from these sessions in other environments. By August 2014 I was writing in her notebook that she was offering begging, bowing, waving her right paw as well as the usual more established left one whilst in the reservoir. And taking in many different places out with the different locations at home was a big part of this as well as our continued focus on her micro moves!

So, what is a micro move? I was clicking and rewarding Dare so often for tiny changes in her body such as shifts in her body weight, and small body movements. These micro moves became the basis for many more tricks and allowed me to interrupt the repetition in her offered behaviours. I also believe this training contributed to a body awareness that surely has helped her cope with the muscular tenseness and stress that she previously suffered with. Dare was becoming mind-body aware.

As with all my dogs, learning remains lifelong, it's something I attribute to their ripe old ages – Dare's first friend here, Skye lived to almost nineteen years old and Dare's other big sister Bonnie kept on learning as she recovered from her stroke and had to relearn how to stand up and then walk. Dare loves the free shaping sessions where she often chooses to repeat her favourite behaviours as that is the kind of girl Dare is, but I try and expand her life experience by encouraging her to offer and repeat new behaviours.

I hope that I enrich Dare's psychological life by offering her the opportunity to be creative, to express herself and make choices and to use Maslow's words to 'self-actualise'.

15 NAPPY NIPPING

When Dare took up residence here I was already aware that she wasn't good with children as she came labelled as a 'nappy nipper'. Her reputation needed a rapid turnaround!

It was clear from my experience with my neighbours' children and my work with Dare on stopping her fence chasing, as well as from our on-lead walks that her interest was more sound based but she was also reactive to their movement to a lesser degree.

This was one of those issues where we could make a start at home in preparation for the real world, and if Dare was able to build a relationship with children in her home environment then it was going to be a great basis for further successes in the big wide world.

I have often thought how difficult socialisation around children would be if I were not a woman! Most of this training was done at our local playing fields and sports centre and whilst walking near schools at break and lunch times. Of course, Dare was always on a lead and I was careful to use distance so that I could ensure Dare would not become so over aroused. I needed to ensure that she would never fail to hear me and that she would always wish to interact with me.

Very quickly Dare was able to sit and watch and was able to do this in close proximity, though I could tell from her antennae ears that she wasn't totally comfortable with the situation.

We worked with play as the reward for watching in these situations where Dare was likely to want to chase such as children at play, football and in particular rugby matches and fast/ lively dogs at play. Dare was quickly able to passively watch and show no signs of lunging or leaning forwards ready to lunge and in return Dare and I would play with her favourite toy. These 'games' she enjoyed so much that whenever I walk near the sports field I am prompted by Dare to return to the game. So, she will look at the children playing football then look at me, and if I am not quick to respond to her game and she has 'asked' for the play and I have ignored her too much she will nudge her nose on my pocket to remind me she deserves the ball!

Dare now enjoys the company of children with the self-control of not nipping or mouthing at them. In some respects, this was the most difficult situation to resolve as I didn't have access to many children for her to meet. And as with so many dogs, this was compounded by the fact that children's' reactions and behaviour are so more varied and unpredictable than most people and their voices more shrill.

I attribute the growth in her confidence and her ability to cope with her sound sensitivities as the main factors in Dare's ability to meet children appropriately. Whilst time and time again I have considered that the early neutering that Dare was highly likely to have been subjected to at the rescue centre is the cause of so many of her problems. Such problems as I have mentioned already from her under confidence, reactivity, bolting to noise phobias are linked to early neutering.

16 PICKING UP MEN

I had been warned that Dare was not good with men, yet it took time for this to manifest itself.

Dare was so very fond of my son and partner and their friends, she had met Michelle's husband and his friends! There had never been any issues. So, there was a part of me thought that this couldn't be an issue and that perhaps someone had been mistaken as Dare had successfully met and interacted with so many men. However, her behaviour towards the man at her first obedience class certainly worried me and I found myself looking for places Dare would encounter men!

I selected football and rugby games as places to visit with Dare and made a point of speaking to any men I met out walking their dog/s.

It became apparent that Dare was fearful of a certain type of man – she seemed to dislike physically stocky/well-built men and she was none too fond of some English accents! Now of course this is a sweeping generalisation as she showed no fear of my friends' English husband and my son is what you could describe a strapping lad! We are always quick to generalise issues such as this so a dog reactive to men will be reactive to all men and noise sensitivity being fear of any loud noises or fireworks as a whole which is often not the case.

This was one of the quickest issues to resolve with Dare and she's shown no fearful reaction to any men we have met for such a long time.

Needless to say, Dare made many male friends who obliged me by scatter feeding her (throwing handfuls of titbits on the ground) and just letting her be in their company for a brief time. Sometimes it was me throwing the food as I chatted to men we'd met whilst out and about on a walk or perhaps on a visit to an event. One event we attended was a

Viking Battle Re-enactment, so the men were a bit 'scary' in their Viking Costumes but quickly Dare was able to sit beside them next to a fire. Little did I know that a couple of years later she was to meet people on a film set dressed in a couple of centuries later costume but having the same feisty battle attitude when she was on set of the Netflix film 'The Outlaw King'.

At some of our regular haunts the men (and of course women and children!) we would meet knew Dare's name but not mine and I have always been touched by the kindness people have shown to her bringing her biscuits and treats, asking where she'd been if we'd missed a week or two and on occasion encouraging their friends to come and meet Dare.

The world truly loves a shaggy dog story!

17 TRIPS TO SHOWS

Of course, life went on for my other dogs too, and we attended shows and naturally Dare came with us. Mainly it was dog dance shows but occasionally we went to an obedience show or perhaps a Bearded Collie Club event.

Dare has always enjoyed the travelling as she's more than happy to be in her cage. Traffic was never a great problem for her either despite the noise next to busy roads and motorways and she was always happy to have a brief toilet break at service stations. I am always looking for something better than a motorway service station for the dogs to walk and enjoy so beaches, parks and even canal walks close to the motorways were very much appreciated too.

Settling in hotel rooms could pose a problem and banging doors, voices and a range of other sounds often proved difficult for her to cope with in the early days. The other difficulty was sleeping with Dare, or rather not sleeping! She was unable to settle at all unless the cage was introduced and the door closed. However, it wasn't long before the cage door remained open, but Dare was happy to go to settle and sleep, and two years later she was able to be in the Travelodge we stayed at Birmingham and was not only relaxed but able to enjoy an après Crufts canine feast from one of our favourite dog delis.

Of course, in the early days I wasn't considering competing with Dare but the environment around a show makes a useful place to socialise and where many people can be counted on for support, help and understanding.

For Dare coping indoors was always more difficult. In the early days she was even fearful of my dog room where she could hear the children next door especially if the windows were open and where she disliked the hanging light. I often felt Dare must have spent little time indoors in the early stages of her life as so many things indoors were not to her liking.

Heelwork to Music shows tend to be indoors so her trips to these shows always consisted of a very brief appearance from Dare. I would take her to the entrance door and reward, take her in and bring her out many times. And in the early days she was hardly in the building for more than a few seconds. I would generally mix and match these ins and outs of the building as much as I felt she could successfully cope with. There was no going in to sit and watch together in the early days!

Obedience and agility shows and the Bearded Collie Club events we attend offered outdoors environments that generally she found more comfortable. In the early days she was a visitor, but I have entered her in a couple of obedience shows though I found she didn't enjoy the environment and my aim was training rather than competing. Despite being solid in stays at home and in class they proved to be a problem at the first show she broke her stays and came creeping up to me, whilst at her the last shows her stays did not prove a problem even with an airport right next to the stay ring. That achievement of Dare being able to stay in such an environment means so very much to me and it was something I for so long wondered if she'd ever achieve! It's important to me that she is happy doing stays and I know that she is not completely comfortable in that situation – her ears twitch, she looks unsettled even though she is not moving and she is clearly very environmentally aware. We are still working on stays and the distraction method I use seems to give her something to focus on. So, who knows perhaps she will return to obedience!

These shows did provide some useful universals that we could transfer into the HTM environment such as the feedback from loud speakers and the high activity level of dogs, all of which we could put distance on with ease and work to bringing Dare into close proximity with.

The unexpected would occasionally rear its ugly head. At one show we regularly attend I was working on getting Dare towards the door when we were flooded by an airplane display such as that the Red Arrows perform. Despite the fact that things at home were starting to settle with the airplanes and helicopters this proved far too much, and her fear was so profound that her return to my van was rapid, with myself on the end of the lead of course. Once in her cage she shrunk to the furthest point at the back looking very small and fearful. Such situations are heart-breaking and feel like mammoth steps back in time, but there is nothing for it but to take a break, drink a coffee and then start afresh having put aside these feelings. Then most importantly try to take even just a few steps forward again, so later that day we made it back to the door, played a lot and then quit while we were ahead!

There were of course other aspects of show environments Dare was fearful of, but there was also a host of things she enjoyed immensely. Dare seemed to enjoy the new environments with their new smells to take in, then there were people who made a fuss of her and fed her different titbits and of course they often had new dog friends to meet and in time play with. All this making for many positive associations around dog shows which I am sure has helped her settle at shows.

18 FREEDOM AND AGILITY

One thing I've always understood about Dare is that she loves to run and needs to run – it transforms her from arousal and worry to a happy and alert dog.

In the early stages of giving her this freedom I was lucky enough to be able to use a couple of fields and other enclosed areas locally which even included a tennis court! The variety of places was very useful with each providing unique distractions and potential worries for Dare, as well as giving us a place to play, learn some tricks and develop some controlled running games.

I was active in Agility over ten years ago in my younger and fitter years and I knew that agility would provide an outlet for Dare's energy and need to move. I was also aware given Dare's interest in active dogs that there was a potential for her to be naughty in an agility class!

I enrolled her with a local agility class where I knew the classes would be indoors and just as importantly small in number. She wasn't to go unaccompanied as her confident little friend Dinky was to go with her.

Dare made rapid progress and learned all of the equipment so very quickly and more importantly she just loved it. She was a demon weaver and was able to flow round courses so very soon into her training. Of course, it was building on her controlled running games and her confidence was boosted to the extent that she rapidly ceased to worry about the barn on windy days.

We started our agility in May 2014 at a point where Dare was unable to do stays in a class situation so one of my aims was to introduce brief periods of stillness to her training such as a wait on the start line, vitally important with a speed demon like Dare and on the contact equipment, the A Frame, Dog walk and see saw. Dare achieved this so very quickly and I have no doubts that it contributed to her growth in confidence and her ability to enjoy periods of stillness.

Dare was always desperate to get into the barn for her training, and only once did she misbehave and take off after another dog with intent to play. Even better she was in no hurry to leave the class and made plenty friends both human and canine when we were their! Over the time we attended agility class I really appreciated how far Dare had come – there was only rarely an uncomfortable and tense reaction from Dare to another dog rather she enjoyed herself with her many new friends.

We don't have time to manage along to class now, however Dare does love it when I bring out our agility equipment and she's certainly not forgotten any of her agility skills.

19 UPS AND DOWNS

Two very important things happened in Dare's life in May 2014– one was hugely upsetting and the other an exciting new idea that would support and scaffold Dare's sounds sensitivities. The common feature of both things was to be a great deal of hard work.

I'll start with my heart stopping story of Dare going missing. This is every dog owner's nightmare and as I write this I can feel every awful emotion I felt that night of Dare's disappearance.

I've always been aware of the power of environment – it's true for myself as I am aware I function better in certain environments and of course it's true for our dogs. For this reason, I take classes not only indoors but outdoors so that in a more distracting and interesting environment we can test our dogs' loose lead walking, recall and other behaviours. Naturally I had done this with Dare and once she would recall reliably in class I had started to let her off lead both on her own and with the others in safe environments. I was so very impressed by her improvement in recall and could even call her out of the herding behaviour she was occasionally showing with my dogs at this time.

Then of course there was the incident I have already mentioned with the Collies on the beach where Dare herded them and had to be returned to onlead briefly. Progress is rarely linear and of course there were ups and downs and a few detours along the way.

I can hardly bear to think about what happened when we all went for a walk at Lanark Loch with Michelle and her dogs after the Bearded Collie Club (Scottish Branch) Heelwork to Music Show. It was later on in the day as we walked the dogs prior to our drive home. We had been walking for about half an hour when suddenly Dare was nowhere to be seen, calling her name was followed by shouting and a rapid trek to my van to see if something had spooked her resulting in her making her way there. Alas there was no sign of her so once the other dogs were safely in their cages I set off leaving Michelle at the van in case Dare should return.

I walked in the dark around this remote loch, the only people I met to ask about Dare were the anglers out for night fishing, but no one had seen her. I have no idea how long I was away, perhaps an hour and back at the van Michelle hadn't seen Dare either.

I started the vans engine, she might hear it and come running. I was starting to fear something could have happened to her and this is not a place she knew as she hadn't walked here before. I phoned the police, reported her missing and still no news.

Both Michelle and I had become hypersensitive to any movement with both of us thinking anything that moved could be Dare and many times I set off to investigate something. I walked around the golf club, around the loch in the complete darkness and even around the restaurant at the gateway.

Just when we were resigned to a night in my van waiting for Dare, she appeared. She was so dirty she was almost unrecognisable. That said she was happy enough and looked none the worse for her adventure and with great relief we could all go home. But before we went home I just could not stop hugging this dirty little girl. I can't tell you how relieved I felt.

Who was more tired the next morning – me or Dare? I am sure it was me! Dare had a bath, and I checked her over and she was absolutely fine. But one thing was for sure she was back on a lead!

It did get me thinking – why was she so dirty? I knew Dare enjoyed digging at home but had never seen her dig anywhere else not at the beach or in either of the fields we walk in or even around the various trails.

One place I had been avoiding walking Dare was the walks right next to Prestwick airport, yet she no longer bothered with the airplanes or helicopters that go over my house, nor did she bother with them out on walks anymore. Perhaps it was time to take a walk here where I knew Dinky enjoyed digging particularly around the rabbit burrows. But, of course Dare was going to be on a long line.

Just as well Dare was on a long line as there is no way I would ever have got her focus off the rabbits here. She watched them, chased as far as she could on the line and much digging ensued. On a positive note she didn't even notice the planes taking off and landing over our heads!

So now I'd seen this, there was work to do and this was to take some time. Dinky had pioneered the rabbit training as she behaved like a terrier about rabbit holes and mole hills and of course my worry was that she would get down a hole and get stuck. So it was like déjà vu to be starting this training over again so quickly after Dinky!

Almost every day I took Dare to any rabbit populated areas I could find on her long line and initially on her own or with her fellow digger, Dinky. Dare is a dog who will offer repetition easily, so it was relatively straightforward to work with her for 10 mins or so. This involved her looking at the holes or sniffing then recalling her to play tuggy with the rabbit skin I had bought for Dinky or to tug and 'kill' on her squeaky toys. Dare had at this point strong self-control behaviour on these toys, in that she could not only leave but watch as I played, squeaked and moved her fur on the end of a whippet / tease toy. I was also able to quickly introduce digging on cue followed by recall to play, and finally she learned to recall to be allowed to dig. So, I had a great new trick based on a natural behaviour, with 'DIGGY' as the chosen cue. Even better it was a very strong behaviour as it was associated with a natural reward which she very much enjoyed.

I am making it sound very easy and of course it did take time for Dare to be able to be off lead in certain environments, especially early morning and evenings when the rabbits were about! In July 2014 I was still working on this when I spent the week in Anglesey, where there were rabbits galore around the beach areas. By this point I could see that only minor progress had been made. Dare was still very aroused in her body posture, tail carriage and those very alert pricked ears, and her focus was on the rabbits and their burrows rather than on the play which was somewhat less powerful compared to her normal strong play.

In the early stages I always kept her line short and stayed close to her, increasing the distance between us even whilst she was on a line took a great deal of time. At each stage I started to allow her to return to dig to test whether I could recall her from her digging. And I am not saying that there weren't set backs and days where she was not interested in stopping digging, days when I gave up and finished a session on a low note, which I so hate to do. However, by early in 2015 when I was in the north of Scotland to take a workshop, we were staying with a friend who has rabbits all around her farmhouse and I had absolutely no issues. I have written in Dare's Diary that Dare was the perfect houseguest and not only was she well behaved in that there was no digging, but she behaved herself so very well with all the Collies we were staying with.

I like my dogs to be able to express their natural behaviours and I have had a few natural diggers over the years. It's always been fairly easy to accommodate by having a place in the garden for digging. For Dare I can't say how confidence building and important it was to allow her to express herself in digging. Of course, part of this was also that she liked to use her nose and we play a lot of scent games, but Dare was about to use her nose in a very different way.

20 THE POWER OF SCENT

What dog doesn't enjoy sniffing and dogs have a great ability to smell......... but of course I don't need to tell you that!

You'll have gathered by now that I had done an incredible amount of desensitisation work with Dare, far more than with any dog I had ever lived with because I had never encountered such a sound sensitive dog before. I don't say that her issues were profound lightly as my first Bearded Collie was so sound sensitive that I had experienced with him a tiled bathroom floor being dug up, carpets scraped till there was no pile, a caravan awning totally destroyed after he escaped from his cage at an agility show and so much more! My beloved Bertie reacted to fireworks, the sound of traffic on wet roads and gunshot. He was by anyone's definition sound sensitive, yet Dare was far more frightened, had a far greater list of fears and her reaction was far stronger than Bertie's.

I had taken time to identify the sounds she was fearful of and draw up lists. These lists were very specific, so I did not simply use the generic fireworks but what aspect of fireworks I felt she was fearful of, so I had on my list sounds such as loud bangs and whoosh sounds! I had done a lot of work with children around playing fields and schools, and of course around my neighbour's children, whom she quickly accepted. I was able to identify the specific sounds that children were making she was reacting to and add these to my very lengthy lists. Of course, the lists could grouped to some extent too so I knew in certain environments that a particular cluster of sounds were most likely to be heard.

I had worked with sound recordings with Bertie with very little success and it's my opinion that the sound does not resonate in the same manner on a recording as it does in the real world. That said I did play these in the house for Dare's benefit and was able to increase the volume over time to a significantly loud sound with little reaction from her. But the real world was another matter!

Dare's confidence was growing with her shaping and trick training, and her recovery rate if something did frighten her was so much faster in most contexts and flight was becoming not necessarily her first reaction to a fear stimulus. So, by May 2014 I was able to write in Dare's diary that I had dropped a whole tray of glasses on the kitchen floor and she bolted back to the hall but came forward towards me almost immediately and also that whilst sitting outdoors she dived indoors at some military planes overhead but came straight back and sat beside me. Of course, as delighted as I was, and I was shouting out loud inside, I remained matter of fact and kept cool and calm with Dare.

Supporting and scaffolding learning and behaviour is very important to me and I was working on trying to ensure the environment was right for learning and that Dare was not going to be flooded or placed in the midst of a fearful situation. I wanted to ensure that the process for teaching her was appropriate and one in which she would be able to learn free of stress and where nothing was being asked of her that she wasn't able to achieve. I was now to introduce to this a new strategy to support and scaffold Dare's learning.

Whilst abroad teaching I met a lady with a Collie with whom I discussed fear and sound sensitivity with over lunch. Of course, communication wasn't easy as her English wasn't very good and my other languages are limited to very poor French, however she planted in my head the idea to counter condition using aromatherapy, something she had successfully used with her Collie. It's so very true in life people and things are placed before us for a reason, and I needed something at this time to support and scaffold Dare to live in the world of sounds she was so frightened of.

I came home and gave what I had been told so much thought. I wasn't aware of the process she had been taken through by the aromatherapist and I spent a few weeks pondering on how I was going to get started. It made such sense to me to use the dogs very powerful sense of smell, often quoted as ten thousand times greater than ours to build positive associations but additionally a dog's world is far more scent based than visual. And my focus had been on the visual and auditory primarily up to this point. I was also aware personally as a less olfactory species, a mere human, that the power and associations that smells hold are so very strong. As such I cannot bear citronella/lemon scents as it reminds me of the first person I knew dying of cancer, when I smell it I can still see the whole scene of the bedroom in which this woman died. By contrast I find the scent of honeysuckle incredibly relaxing and joyous as I grew up spending time surrounded by this scent in several houses from ones I lived in (with a keen gardener in my mother) and a house I holidayed in with my aunt.

I started working on this in May of 2014 and It was work in progress for some time. It started with shopping, I had decided to purchase a selection of aromatherapy oils and headed off to our local health shop. I didn't consult any books on aromatherapy and tried to put out of my head any conventional wisdom of what oils are supposed to do! As I've said already our personal associations may override this so lavender is not relaxing for me rather it is associated with the death of my grandmother. I could not possibly know what associations with scent that Dare may hold. I selected the oils randomly – Lavender, Patchouli, Eucalyptus, Rose, Oregano, Rosemary, Peppermint and Frankincense. And of course, since I had no way of knowing what experience Dare had of any of these smells what I was about to look for was what her choices and preferences would be.

I had a plan for how I was going to let Dare select her oil and in this I found a new use for my scent cloths from obedience, though you could easily use cotton handkerchiefs. I picked eight clean cloths which I was not going to handle by hand only with tongs, and between uses would be stored in their separate sealed bags. Each bag I labelled with the oil name and placed a cloth with around ten drops of the oil on into each bag. So, I was ready to start and was wondering what Dare would make of this new activity.

On the first day, I put all of the other dogs away and spent time with Dare just sitting in the conservatory, feeding her and making sure she was calm. Outside I'd placed the cloths out on the ground and surrounded each cloth with four little titbits. The idea was that she'd investigate each cloth as she'd eat the titbits surrounding them and that is exactly what she did! She didn't seem to pay much attention to the cloths but just returned to me where we sat a while. She showed no further interest in the cloths and so less than ten minutes later I was putting the cloths away in the appropriate bags with my tongs while Dare chewed a lamb rib in the conservatory!

I repeated the same procedure every day, if it was raining I brought the same scenario indoors and we did it in the dog room. The order of the cloths going out was random and there was no order she could be feeding into. On Day Eight I was still placing my four pieces of identical food around the cloths, but she started to show more interest in the cloths after eating. This was a first and exactly what I was hoping for and though I wanted to cheer out loud I kept quietly excited.

She didn't exactly look like a dog at Crufts doing a scent exercise, she looked more like a dog sniffing in the grass at various points. I'd be sitting watching and I started to have a pen and paper at the ready and was tally marking how many times she went back to a give smell and noting if she spent any length of time investigating any of the cloths. but this continued for another two weeks before my little tally marks next to my numbered cloths revealed that she never went back to the Eucalyptus or Peppermint oils. So, I felt safe in discarding two of my cloths.

I kept going with the daily and sometimes twice daily exercises and tried to make sure I did them at different times of the day – I didn't want her to be influenced by different states such as hunger or tiredness, for example. They didn't take long to carry out and over time I was able to whittle away the cloths till I was left with three oils – Lavender, Rose and Patchouli. It took me some time to get down to a favourite, and finally it was clear that Dare preferred the patchouli, on several occasions she even picked up this cloth and when I ignored her she on all bar one occasion lay down with it. I asked myself did I influence the choice in any way but if I had I would not have selected this oil!

So far, this process had taken me over a month and now the real work was to begin. I had bought Dare cotton baby bandanas, which I felt would hold the scent far better than the perhaps prettier ones that can be bought for dogs. And I was ready with the patchouli scented baby bibs in their bags all set to go.

By this time, I had identified a lot of activities that Dare really enjoyed. There were the many games of football she played both on her own but also with the other girls, there was agility training, tearing out the toyboxes and playing with the toys especially the noisy toys, the trips to the beach, chewing on a bone and so on! Dare was to wear her scented bandanas in these settings and in doing so the scent of patchouli would become associated with so very many positive experiences. And I watched on, enjoying seeing her happy and hoping the next stage would be as successful!

The next stage was a huge leap of faith for me as I had done so much preparation to reach it, indeed truth be told I had put it off and put it off! What I now had to do was start to take our patchouli bandanas into settings where Dare was likely to be unsure, fearful or/and sound sensitive! I want to just stress this didn't mean I was going to flood her just use the scent to support her to cope with the work I had already started of getting Dare to look at and be on the periphery of feared environments.

I decided to be brave and off we went to the playing fields where Dare reacted to the sound of the children's voices especially if they were shrill, the battering of balls off the metal fencing, the sound of certain men's' voices, I could go on! I parked in the car park in the quietest spot and waited for Dare to show an interest in coming out, in fact she was quick to come out as soon as she saw the bandana. On went the bandana and Dare started out more positively than usual. The session was successful, in my opinion more so than usual with Dare showing no signs of fear or reactivity. Needless to say, I was on a huge high and Dare looked a happy girl!

Now there were the a few setbacks but as I have already said progress is rarely without the occasional stumble! One of the biggest scares Dare had while wearing her bandana took place in August 2014 when we attended a heelwork to music show to socialise Dare around the outside of the building. There was an air show in the area and these fast planes were going over our heads, Dare was petrified and dragged me back to the van where she wanted the safety of her cage. I was just about to close the door when it struck me she wasn't at the very back of the cage cowering as would usually happen, so I turned my back on the cage and just sat leaving both her lead on but the door of the cage open. It wasn't long before she was out and joining me for a cuddle .... was this incredibly fast recovery the power of the bandana, I believe so.

So, improvements were happening on the sound sensitivity front! Dare had gone from a dog who was readily terrified of so very many sounds which would leave her bolting for safety and then shut down in her cage to a girl who could bolt on fewer occasions, but when she did she could recover very rapidly.

I have often said how amazing and brave Dare is, how quickly she learns, and this is true on all counts. However, I have rarely met a dog as fearful and reactive as Dare and I was in awe of what she was able to achieve.

21 THE THREE AMIGOS, AND OTHER FRIENDS

I have talked a lot about Dare's relationships with my own dogs and I do believe that they played a big role in rehabilitating Dare and building her confidence. But there were other canine influences at play in Dare's life.

Dare had progressed from the fearful dog who avoided contact with other dogs. I still clearly see the girl who in the early days couldn't do enough to avoid contact with dogs, strongly looking away or turning away and showing so many signs of stress as she did so. Then there was the freezing where she was clearly going to fly for safety or get involved in a fight situation. All of this was evident from the day I picked her up and from meeting not only my girls on that day but Gill Crawford and Andrea Rogers' dogs in the car park outside the Travelodge in Birmingham.

In the early days it was almost as if she needed permission to play. Even with her best friend in these days, Skye, where she'd look at me uncertainly as if for permission to play. There was such a hesitancy in her early play, this checking behaviour to see how I was reacting, and she was never assertive. Poor Dare was a bit of a push over in so many situations.

There were other dogs out with our home she was meeting and starting to play with. She was showing playful behaviour at her agility training where she was clearly more aroused and therefore not looking so tense and fearful. We regularly met friends and even client's dogs and Dare was starting to come out of her shell a little, though there was still a hesitancy in her play.

Of course, it helps build a relationship if you see your friends regularly!

She was very fond of Michelle's Bichon Frise, Jaxon. He's a confident dog and though outdoors they didn't play much, when Jaxon came to stay with me on holidays they often lay sleeping together. But when Michelle got her Bearded Collie, Luna a new relationship was to be built. Luna was a confident and assertive puppy and initially it wasn't love at first sight as Dare was terrified of her and reverted to looking away, acting submissive and generally being mugged ... or should it be thugged! But confident dogs are good for Dare and it wasn't long before they were close buddies and she would reject her sisters to play solely with Luna.

Luna has been a big part of Dare's life since those early days. And as time has went on it's become evident that when they play together it's like she sees and hears nothing to worry about. There play is rarely disturbed by anything going on, even if it's going on very close by. I have never underestimated the power and ability of dogs to assist with the rehabilitation and learning of other dogs and I have always believed and indeed witnessed dogs learning from each other. With these two together that was so very apparent. It has become a play of equals, with the turn around from Dare's fear of Luna coming when she actually ticked Luna off for thugging her – there was growling, Dare pushed her over and it all happened so very quickly, and what remained was a strong friendship.

In August 2015 Luna's sister from a repeat mating came to live with us. She was just as confident as her sister and so was named for the little know it all that she was, Google. Luna had already established a relationship with Google in our visits to the litter before they went to their new homes, and fitting in as if she had never left! Google and Dare immediately hit it off and their relationship followed a similar pattern to that with Luna.

Anyone who follows my photographs on social media can see that these three are always together and we've named them as the Three Amigos. They play together, they chill and relax together and they even train well together. Dare has grown and developed a certain bravery in the company of these bombproof and confident sisters.

It's almost impossible to take Dare anywhere without her winning hearts and influencing people. She's so very special and loving! But Dare is able to win over other dogs too and I have had great success using her to meet with some of my behavioural clients. She has a way with small dogs and dogs who show signs of fear as well as being able to work with the more confident and difficult characters we meet. She's developed and uses good dog communications skills, she plays appropriately, and in my opinion and experience it's rare to have a dog that works well with almost any other dog type.

22 MOVING ON UP

Dare did not come into my life to compete and I had no aspirations to compete with her in our early days together. It was too far flung a prospect that she would ever be able to cope in a competition setting. She came into my life accidentally and she captured my heart very early on. I described her as many things she was my behavioural work in progress, she was my challenge in life as I always need a challenge and my ambition for her was that she would be a happy girl who enjoyed life!

Of course, I had taken Dare along to shows where she had kept us company, and I had used the show environment to socialise her. On the whole she coped very well in the car park areas and with the other dogs and of course people. And she enjoyed all the new smells and different walks that accompanied these expeditions. There were areas that required a lot of work and I spent a great deal of time taking her to the feared doors and taking through these doors, bringing her out and repeating this a few times over the course of our day. My aim of course was to get her comfortable and inside the buildings that most shows we attended took place in, but I had a lot of work to do to achieve this. The outdoor shows and events we attended helped immensely and provided easier ways to help Dare cope with things such as loudspeakers. We could position ourselves far away and move closer and use the external rewards that Dare enjoyed such as sniffing around in long grass and playing with her toys.

I was fortunate enough that a friend got me the use of a sports hall and I took Dare along. The acoustics in sports halls I knew were a difficulty for Dare and I was lucky in that I managed several sessions where it was just Dare and I in a very large sports hall! The format for these sessions was pretty much the same so included letting her take in the silence in our hall and the noises from out with, playing with our favourite toys and eating the very tastiest of titbits and listening to music played through speakers at ever increasing volumes. She took this in her stride, I expected there would be problems rather this was a resounding success!

So, my aim in entering Dare at a show was not to compete but to see if she was able to focus and cope in a buildings environment. Of course, not all buildings echo and resonate sound in the same manner but I had done my very best to help her cope with this environment prior to entering and I felt that this would be a test of how far she had progressed.

So, let's begin the whistle stop tour of Dare's journey to the top and it started in Blackpool!

I always really enjoyed Blackpool show so it was an obvious place to start. Good associations for me and a happy me would definitely be helpful for Dare. By this time Dare had made fleeting appearances indoors at shows where she ate a lot of titbits and did very little else. I was not hugely optimistic and almost didn't bother to take her into the ring. There had been a banging door that had frightened her earlier in the day and though we had walked past it a few hours earlier and she showed no sign of bolting I could see her recognition of the fear she'd felt their earlier on. However, in all other ways the day had went smoothly enough with Dare enjoying running in the field to the rear of the show and meeting her friends both canine and human, and of course I had handed in her music at the beginning of the day – though this was an irrelevancy as I had a plan and the music was simply background noise!

Michelle was able to keep me informed as to the progression of Dare's class and when it was our turn. This allowed me to super charge Dare's confidence by playing with her favourite toys out on the grass and then enter the building and find our way to the warm up area to wait for our turn in the ring. All went swimmingly well, she was so keen to get into the building and she was very focused on me and her toy. My plan was going well and when we were welcomed into the ring, off we went with Dare on her loose and light weight lead and myself with Dare's toy hidden on my person. My plan was to keep Dare moving for the most part and to play with her for more than half of our time. She was so settled and unperturbed by the whole experience that I dropped her lead and was able to throw in her favourite distraction game where I squeak her ball under my foot and she has to ignore it, stay in heel and wait for her click word to take the toy. We had played throughout our three and a half minutes but I wanted to finish by throwing the ball around and so did this just before the music was due to stop a few times. When the music finished Dare didn't want to leave the ring as she was so busy enjoying her toy which of course elicited laughter from the audience, but for my part I was just so thrilled with how the experience had went. This was a dream result and I had wet eyes (yes, that's tears!)!

She had three very frightened experiences in the week following this show, the worse of which was our neighbours Land Rover which was making some seriously unhealthy sounding banging noises which saw her bolt into her cage where it took her some time to recover and reappear. She had been so much more settled at home and this was THE most important thing as far as I was concerned. There were also two incidents relating to my classes, the first where she wouldn't come out of her cage for Michelle and the second where the closing up noises from the garage next door which she had by this time become accustomed to send her bolting for the exit.

I seriously considered not taking her back in the ring as I was concerned that I might be destroying the hard work we had done together and that the three incidents in the following week may have been some form of stress related deterioration. I just wanted to cosset her and keep her safe at home I guess! I am thankful that I was sent a video of Dare's training round and could see that she was happy, and committed to do what was asked of her, albeit very little, and most importantly that she was really enjoying herself and showing this by her confident play, her wagging tail and her big sticky up ears, which go back when she is frightened, in fact her whole being said HAPPY. This and the quick recovery rate she was in most instances showing after incidents made the decision for me not to quit on Competition Dog Dare.

I had plenty time between this experience and Westglen's popular and busy show in October 2014 to work on a heelwork routine and competing. I chose Heelwork to keep her confident and close, where she likes to be and she really had so very few moves that the easiest option was to put together a basic Novice routine. I am not a pressured handler and don't feel stressed ever, so there was no way that I was going to cause stress to Dare and all I hoped for in return was that she would do her best. And I knew Dare would always do her best for me!

The show came around all so quickly and we had been away for a week whilst I was working, so there had been very little time for training Dare and her routine! The music I had selected was Saddle Up by David Christie where I was a cowboy and Dare my sidekick! Dare really performed so very well with her music and we won her first Novice class on the first day and was pipped into second place on the second day. I watched her on video afterwards, such a happy and committed performance and if I had smell-o-vision the scent of patchouli would have engulfed us! So, by March 2015 at the same venue near Birmingham Dare got her second novice heelwork win and we moved on up to Intermediate! This was like a birthday present – taking place only a year after picking Dare up at Crufts.

It's relatively easy to progress through classes in the UK in HTM and by our next show in May at Blackpool Dare had moved up a class and was in Intermediate HTM. I hadn't altered the routine as I felt it was important to consolidate what she had already learned and build her confidence. I wanted her to feel confident in the ring environment so that she would be able to achieve what she was able to work on with ease in our training sessions.

The first class of the day was her Intermediate HTM and to my delight it was a resounding win with Dare working so very well. I couldn't have asked for more than this continuing progress, but more importantly I couldn't have asked for a more confident and committed performance!

Meanwhile I had decided that given all the work Dare had been doing on controlled running to motivate, reward and destress that this would transfer so readily into a freestyle routine! Dare really enjoyed these activities and so I constructed and choreographed a fluid routine filled with movement and very few pauses which offered Dare the perfect opportunities to run! I also picked a theme which I felt suited her scruffy 'urchin' looks, she was to be the gypsy's dog with myself as the gypsy. The uncomfortable one in this partnership was myself as wearing a dress is not something I do very often! I knew this was the perfect choreography for Dare both in terms of the movement to motivate and the combination of light and shade when combined with the static poses, and I couldn't wait to see how it all came together in the ring!

I take full advantage of every opportunity to train in the ring, as I have said every environment is different especially for sensitive dogs. So, on the first day I trained Dare in her Novice Freestyle and was so very pleased with her that on the second day she worked the class and won! However, she still got a play in the ring as I decided that she could train and play her heelwork class. It was early days and I wanted her to enjoy her time in the ring as in my opinion that's the basis for a performance worked with commitment and drive. I love all my dogs to ooze joy when they are performing!

Our next show was only a week later and was in Lanark. Another win in Novice Freestyle took Dare and her gypsy routine into Intermediate. I was so very pleased with her performance and was starting to see routes to take in her training, ways to progress and the distance work was confident, clean and accurate. I was getting to know Competition Dare.

And let's not forget the heelwork class, where Dare really was clearly the girl on fire and her Intermediate win took her to Advanced. It felt slightly unbelievable that she had achieved this much and so very quickly. Of course, as far as Dare was concerned it was all about the things she enjoyed doing and the treats and play that went alongside this!

It would have been all too easy to push Dare as she was clearly very talented, but it was time to take stock before our next show. I am not a pushy trainer, so I decided to review what we had and improve and consolidate this, rather than make radical changes or choreograph a more complex routine in her Freestyle. I was still working on changes when we went to Wales for Y Mons show in July. She won both Intermediate Freestyle classes and put in a sound performance in the HTM Qualifier attaining 6th place with her four heelwork positions routine (there are eight positions in total). It was time for a new routine if we were to seriously compete in the Advanced class and of course I had been working on a few additional positions. Dare was picking these up very rapidly but of course they were all up close and she really loves being close to me. But I needed to ensure she was confident in these, so I would not let Dare down by allowing her to become confused or unsure in anything that happened in the ring.

Our next show of 2015 was back at Blackpool again, and my aim here was to focus on Dare and Dinky. Dare's win her in Intermediate Freestyle took us to Advanced Freestyle and my work in the background on a new Heelwork routine was not ready to be outed. Dare needed time to become confident in all her new heelwork positions.

It's a long journey to Leicester for me but I decided to attend Canine Freestyle GB's show here in September 2015. I had both Dare and Gertie in the Advanced Freestyle Qualifier, which was divided into two parts – with both girls winning their parts! Dare's beautiful new routine appropriately about finding her way to the beach taking second place in the HTM Qualifier – she'd qualified in both HTM and Freestyle.

There are just no words to express my joy and excitement at what Dare had done but more than anything my amazement at what this girl was capable of learning!

We attended the Crufts Semi Finals at Rugby in chilly January 2016. Another new environment to take on board and she took it in her stride. She took fifth place in the Freestyle Qualifier and this meant Dare would not only go to Crufts but represent Scotland in the International Freestyle.

23 PREPARING FOR CRUFTS

It was such early days for Dare who'd been competing for only just over a year. Without doubt she would be the least experienced dog there but she had earned her place, so I had to put aside all of these thoughts and focus on supporting Dare.

Crufts is a very hard environment to work towards competing in. There were the obvious differences between the shows she'd already been to and performing in the much larger main arena with its massive crowds, cameras, and so forth. Apart from this there was the crowds of people and the acoustics of the large halls in the Exhibition Centre in Birmingham. So many of these things were unknown quantities to Dare and some were experiences I could not replicate for her to experience ahead of the show.

What I intended was to do my very best to plan ahead and ensure Dare was as happy as possible in this huge venture we were going to undertake together. And to do this I was going to put aside the Gypsy routine which she would be performing - there's no point in going over and over a routine with any dog as in some respects the routine is the easy part and she knew it so very well!

So, I recommended the confidence building games and took them to various places and we not only played but we spent time on Dare's other favourite activity, cuddling! We visited all kinds of places from sports centres to football matches, theatres to pubs and music concerts. So, Dare was being exposed to throngs of people, a variety of noise types and of course we did some travelling on public transport. I think Dare was starting to relish these outings as mainly she got to go on her own, and of course she has always enjoyed the attention of people we meet, and we met plenty of people who were happy to make a fuss of her.

Impressively things went so very well and there were no major worries from Dare. She seemed to be taking things in her stride. I added into our visits a few trips to a training ground with AstroTurf. Dare has sensitive pads just like her 'sister' Skye who I first competed at Crufts in Dog Dancing with and I wanted to be sure that she would be fine at Crufts. Dare moves at such great speed and I wanted to make sure she could keep traction on this surface and not be slipping too much. So, we played and did our routine a couple of times!

Dare's life in all other ways continued as it always had with here with plenty of long walks on the beach or in the woods nearby and of course there were visits to her friends and their dogs.

24 REVISITING CRUFTS IN 2016

It was to be Dare's second Gotcha Day, I had picked her up from Nicky only two years earlier. And who could have expected her to be celebrating at Crufts.

The journey to Crufts went well and Dare certainly was a keen traveller. We travelled with Gertie who was also competing in the Heelwork to Music and of course Michelle had come along to help ….

We arrived at our Travelodge, revisiting the car park where Dare was terrified of the airplanes only two years earlier. But this time there was no sign of fear and she was even able to go inside the Travelodge itself!

Having had a quiet night, we set off early on Thurs 6th March for the Exhibition Centre. It was a pleasant walk from the car park accompanied by Dare and Gertie and of course our bags of the things we needed to see us through the day. The Thursday at Crufts is usually a little quieter than the other days, so this was perfect for allowing Dare a gentle introduction and she settled in her cage at her bench. She was eating her titbits, enjoying saying hello to her friends and was so very settled!

When it came for time for her to go outside to pee before competing, it meant a trip to the back door where I had picked her up two years before. It crossed my mind that she might be worried by the planes or trains as we walked along the limited grassy area however I had no reason to worry as she was settled and just enjoyed sniffing about. Dare was indeed daring, and I was humbled by her ability to transform herself (perhaps with a little help!) into the Super girl which the sticker on her harness says she is!

We sat and relaxed in the area behind the main arena waiting for our turn to grace the green carpet. I told myself we could do it together and when we went out into the main arena I felt we were together and as one. Dare fell into her flat on her side position when I asked her, and I left her to take my seat at our 'fire' prop and to 'warm' my hands. A dog with fear or lack of confidence would never have done this and as the story unfolded, Dare brought me a bracelet to wear and the dance then ensued as the pace of the music picked up. As the music calmed and slowed again Dare and I returned to the fire to finish the routine. As I type this I can feel the tears on my cheeks as indeed I did on the day when our routine ended.

We didn't win with this, Dare's first and simple but beautiful routine but we were a creditable sixth place and it was clear that Dare had so much more to offer.

Michelle had been watching on the screen in the area behind the arena and had picked up something so very interesting which is testament to the intelligence and creativity that Dare clearly has in abundance. Whilst performing I had been aware that Dare's usually accurate distance work was a little briefer in length than usual and I had wondered if she had felt less confident, though certainly she was as fast as usual! What Michelle had picked up on was that Dare was actually going around the circular spotlights on the arena floor. When I watched the performance back on video, she was so right. Dare was making sense of and responding to her environment in a way she never would have been able to only two years earlier!

Dare was to get a rest and take a back seat while Gertie performed on Friday and she would be back in the main arena on Saturday. She was enjoying the attention, the company, the walks and of course the deli dinners.

On Saturday Dare had very special visitors come to see her, Rachel's Dad, Tony and her sister Sally had come to Crufts to see her. I am so honoured to have Rachel's Dare and to have taken her to Crufts as she had hoped to do one day.

We were to perform our Gypsy routine in the International Freestyle and we were in the company of some of the best dog dancers from all around the world. There were so many people filling the halls around Crufts and the main arena was full but best of all Dare was taking it all in her stride. She was wearing her patchouli oil dabbed on her collar, she was enjoying the best of titbits and she was playing with her favourite ball and of course I was getting plenty of cuddles!

So, things were going to plan as we stood under the arch waiting to be introduced into the main arena then something happened which had never happened before, a spotlight came towards us! Dare initially behaved as if she was glued to the spot and for one fleeting second, I thought that she would bolt, and of course she wouldn't have been the first dog that was worried by some aspect of the main arena or competing therein.

I called her name and she showed me the trust that she clearly feels and joined me ready to start her routine. She worked through her routine and I was so proud of her and truth be told a little guilty for being the person in our partnership who had felt doubt, albeit fleetingly. We were far from being in the top three, where I have been on several occasions before but the pride I felt in Dare was a feeling I have rarely experienced even when I have been standing at Crufts holding a red rosette!

Such was Dare's Second Gotcha Day, her second birthday with me. We celebrated with Dog Deli Dinner and titbits galore in our hotel room. Dare enjoying a romp with her friends Luna and Jaxon and fellow celebrant, Gertie!

On our journey home we visited the same beach at Lytham St Anne's that we had visited two years earlier on the way to Dare's new Scottish home. Little did I think it would end in Dare staying with me!

25 BEYOND SUCCESS - WHAT DARE DID NEXT!

I am always looking for new challenges and clearly Dare is a girl after my own heart, so we were to find some new challenges to undertake together in the years to come.

The remainder of 2016 offered me many new ways to move forward with Dare. We were still competing together, and of course my other dogs were also joining us at shows and strutting their stuff too. However, I was invited to judge at Crufts for the second time in 2017 so had no need to qualify. That said, with ease Dare would have qualified in both HTM and Freestyle from her many placings at the few shows we managed to attend. And her ability to work in the ring with her greater experiences just grew and grew and new and more complex routines evolved.

On a personal level and inspired by judging the Open European Championships in 2014 at Stuttgart I decided I'd like to compete abroad and have the new challenge of competing against the best competitors from across the world. Late in 2015 The Scottish Kennel Club had given consent to a Team Scotland attending this event which has raised the profile of HTM in Scotland and generated interest in the sport as well as some new and talented handlers.

The Event was to take place in Austria in 2016 and fundraising for this saw a variety of events which gave Dare a host of new experiences. One of the most exciting events was a Gala Dinner in the beautiful Best Western Strathaven Hotel where the entertainment was dog and dance themed. The Tables were named after Scottish dancing dogs so there was even a Dare table! The evening commenced with Penny Mansfield's Australian Shepherd opening proceedings by appearing on the ballroom dance floor, seating herself at a table and ringing the bell, which was the cue for her to be joined by Penny and her other Aussie, Flurry, Michelle and Luna, Marie Docherty and Erin and my own Gertie, Dinky and of course Dare. The meal was fabulous, further entertainment included Lynn Barber from Dogs Trust as a guest speaker, street dancing from Claire Campbell and her crew and even more dancing from the dogs including Dare who danced to some Romanian Gypsy music and got the audience clapping along.

There were other events Dare was now becoming part of. She had attended many demonstrations such as at Agricultural shows and now was taking part alongside my other dogs and of course her other canine friends. This provided a host of new distractions from livestock to vintage cars and tractors! Then there were the Cabaret Evenings which we were hosting as fundraisers and Dare was a busy girl through these showing off her ever-increasing range of moves!

Late in 2016 I was contacted by our agent regards some filming. This always sounds very glamorous, but the reality is a lot of hard work and hanging around waiting for your call. On top of that there is usually a great deal of repetition as scenes are filmed over and over again till the director gets what he wants! I am a massive fan of Diana Gabaldon's Outlander books and was so pleased to hear that this was what I was being asked to be part of, rather not me but my hairy Scottish dogs. Dare was picked alongside Gertie and Google and I was very honest as to my concerns about whether she'd cope with all that would be going on. As it happens she coped very well with being on set and with all the preparation to be a street dog, though sadly she wasn't needed for the filming. I am still in awe of her coping with the clattering of metal poles and rigging and all else that was going on. But for sure she enjoyed her time on set, the company of the other dogs and the attention that a dog on set gets!

Another achievement lay in Dare helping people, how appropriate for a girl who just loves people! I was asked if I would like to be involved in Alzheimer's Dog Days and pay a visit to entertain at a local day centre.

Dare and Dinky were the first to visit and both enjoyed it greatly. Dare certainly knows how to work a room, she enjoys being made a fuss of and of course we do some tricks and a short dance routine. I really hope that my dogs, and Dare make the difference in the lives of these people that my dogs made in the life of my Dad prior to his death.

26 MOVING ON

Sadly, Kennel Cough meant that Team Scotland did not manage to attend the Open European Championships in Austria but last year we made it to Belgium to compete and Dare was to represent Scotland by performing both in Heelwork to Music and in Freestyle. We had made a few trips on ferries to Scottish Islands, visiting Cumbrae, Arran and Mull and the big journey sailing from Newcastle to Amsterdam posed no problem at all to Dare.

The competition took place over four days and Dare was there every step of the way. She was just outside the top ten in the Freestyle, however in the Heelwork performing to the Civil Wars version of Billie Jean Dare took us to the finals in this prestigious competition. We are currently looking forward to competing in Switzerland at the next Open European Competition. Who knows what successes that will bring!

There are plenty of demonstrations and Cabarets which Dare will be appearing at. She's currently working on a routine performed with myself with her Amigos Luna and Google and they are having a lot of fun helping me with the choreography. Oh, how my dogs are the most creative of choreographers ... but I would never have guessed Dare had such things to contribute in those early days!

There was another visit to a film set. This time to the Netflix film, The Outlaw King, a historical film about Robert the Bruce. I think Dare has seen most things now from highlanders with swords in battle, knights on horses, fire and pyrotechnics and even more farmyard animals. Can I just say, she took it all in her stride and I am almost certain she thinks she has the starring role in whatever we do!

Meantime Dare has both qualified for the Crufts Semi Finals in both Heelwork to Music and in Freestyle with her fabulous new routines, so we are thinking ahead to 2019 too!

But these things are Dare and I share as our hobby together. Most of our life is spent in other activities. We enjoy walks where Dare is off lead, often with other dogs and without the avoidance and fear she used to experience. Dare will continue to help me out with my work as a behaviourist in her role as super stooge dog. She really doesn't care if she is barked or lunged at, though I think her talent lies in playing with other fearful dogs and bringing them out of their shells. I guess she understands them.

As I have already said, Dare indulges me in one of my other hobbies, photography. I love that the girl with ants in her pants is now transformed into a poser, my very own super model. She just loves to jump on a chair, put her feet onto a tree stump, and in short find just the right place to stop and pose in the hope that I produce a camera and take her picture. After all there may be a tasty titbit or an interesting game or toy following the click of the camera!

27 THIS IS NOT THE END

My journey with Dare is not at an end.

We have come a long way in terms of her growth in confidence and the joy of life that she exudes but I am not going to say she is 'cured'. Sound sensitivity is a hardwired and adaptive characteristic which may never leave a dog BUT Dare has the most incredible recovery rate and ability to learn and overcome her fears.

Together Dare and I have forged a connection, formed a relationship which I call love. We have a daily ritual of cuddling which she adores, and it is accompanied by my ruffling her fuzzy fur as I tell her how much I love her. For her part I am sure she trusts me and loves me. I have been concerned that she has been a little unsettled when I have been away for more than a few days and I was so very concerned when I was unwell earlier this year that she was refusing to leave me. And as such I am concerned that the down side of such a bond is a little anxiety at my absence, despite her being at home with her Dad and the others. Clearly despite Dare's many, many friends both human and canine we have a very special bond together.

She has learned to cope with her sound sensitivity to an incredible extent which I most certainly didn't anticipate. As I am writing this Scotland has been hit by dreadful weather in the form of two storms in quick succession. The windy weather that only three years ago would have saw Dare run off to hide in her cage has had no impact on her whatsoever. She has simply continued playing around, chewing her bones and toys and her day to day life of walks, games and training hasn't been impacted in the slightest. Indeed, we have had fireworks being let off near us which she has had no reaction to despite these being such a fear factor for her in the early days, where she most certainly would have bolted if she heard them.

As we were out walking yesterday I saw her take in the sound of fireworks which were coming from the sports arenas in the playing fields only a couple of hundred yards away. She acknowledged the sound with her radar ears going back and a slight pause in her play, she turned to look at me and continued on with her toy. I confess that I stopped breathing but only for a whisper! Sound sensitivity is a hardwired, adaptive behaviour in so many instances so her recovery rate has become astounding and this is, rather than aiming for a cure that what I would encourage anyone reading this to work towards if you have a sound sensitive dog.

Dare believes in giving back and helping others who are in a situation which she understands. To that end she has helped me out with my work as a behaviourist where there is no sign of the old Scaredy Dare and she is more than happy to act as a stooge dog and especially enjoys playing with other fearful dogs. I have often wondered if we are attracted to dogs like ourselves or if perhaps our dogs learn our characteristics, or indeed vice versa - I've seen in Dare so many of my characteristics as a person from positivity, belief in change, bravery to this 'giving back' not only in this situation but in so many others. And of course, in giving back, she has given me so much and over a few difficult periods in my life.

So, what will Dare's future hold? Well we have plenty coming up to look forward to including fundraising activities such as Cabaret Evenings for the next Team Scotland which hopefully if selected Dare will be a part of once again. And of course, there is no doubt we will continue to enjoy our dog dancing together at shows in the UK as well as on far more occasions in the local parks and on the beach. But these things are Dare and my hobbies together. Most of our life is spent in other activities such as enjoying time together walking where Dare is off lead, often with other dogs and without the avoidance and fear she used to experience. She has become quite the poser for my photographs indulging me in one of my other hobbies. And these little things give me so much pleasure, I only hope that I give Dare even half as much pleasure as she gives me.

I have a few final words to bring Dare's Diary to a close .... This is not the end!

ABOUT THE AUTHOR

Picture by Andrew Cawley

Heather has a lifetime experience with dogs and has also competed and trained in a variety of canine activities. Over the last thirteen years she has been active in Heelwork to Music, also known as Dog Dancing, in which she has had seven advanced Freestyle dogs and six who have been Advanced in both HTM and Freestyle. Heather is also a three times Crufts winner and Open European Championships finalist.

Heather currently lives in Troon in Scotland with her five dogs. She works as a Behaviourist and Dog Trainer where her work takes her around the UK as well as abroad.

23018327R00064

Made in the USA
Columbia, SC
05 August 2018